W9-CRH-565

The JoyPowered™ Team

By Erin Brothers, JoDee Curtis, Peggy Hogan,
Denise McGonigal, Laura North,
Susan Tinder White, and Liz Zirkelbach

© 2019 by Erin Brothers, JoDee Curtis, Peggy Hogan, Denise McGonigal, Laura North, Susan Tinder White, and Liz Zirkelbach

All rights reserved. No portion of this book may be reproduced, stored in a retrieval system, or transmitted in any form or by any means, including photocopying, recording, or other electronic or mechanical methods, without the prior written permission of the publisher.

Erin Brothers, JoDee Curtis, Peggy Hogan, Denise McGonigal, Laura North, Susan Tinder White, and Liz Zirkelbach do not claim to be employed by, affiliated with, or sponsored by Gallup®. All non-Gallup® information has not been approved and is not sanctioned or endorsed by Gallup® in any way. Opinions, views, and interpretations of Gallup® research are solely the beliefs of the authors of this book.

ISBN 978-1-54397-015-9

Dedicated to our JoyPowered™ team, our families, and our clients!

TABLE OF CONTENTS

"Every breath we take, every step we make, can be filled with peace, joy, and serenity."

- Thich Nhat Hanh

Introduction

This is the third in a series of JoyPowered™ books. The first, *JoyPowered™: Intentionally Creating an Inspired Workspace*, was published in 2016; *The JoyPowered™ Family,* co-written with Denise McGonigal, was released in early 2018.

As our team discussed the idea of JoyPowered™ book number three, we threw out several different ideas. One of the consultants on the Purple Ink team, Stacy, suggested, "How about JoyPowered™ team, and the team could write it?". Hmmm…I was so intrigued and excited, but also nervous about the idea of writing as team. What if we had very different styles? What if I didn't like someone's chapter? What if they didn't like mine? What if someone didn't finish by the deadline? Denise and I had worked together on *The JoyPowered™ Team* easily, but seven of us?

Thankfully, those concerns didn't materialize. I was embarrassed I even had any concerns. It was truly the power of a JoyPowered™ team that made it work beautifully. Not only did we meet deadlines, we exceeded them; we were candid about our questions, praises, and concerns about each other's writing; we collaborated through issues when there was disagreement, and we all focused on the goal – to write

joy*powered*

a book that would help others experience joy when working on a team.

CliftonStrengths®

Although our team is enthusiastic about CliftonStrengths® and we recommend it to everyone we do business with, this book is not just about CliftonStrengths®. The power of understanding what you do best and what your team does best, though, is undeniable. The CliftonStrengths® (also known as StrengthsFinder®) assessment is a quick, easy, inexpensive way to discover your strengths.[1]

If you don't take the CliftonStrengths® assessment, thoughtfully and intentionally consider times when you performed at your highest level, had success, and felt energized. Identify what was driving you when that happened. Your strengths are not about *what* you do, they're about *what drives you* when you are doing it. Although we refer to strengths many times in this book, we also address ways our team and clients have created JoyPowered™ teams with or without a formal understanding of CliftonStrengths®.

For Gallup's short definitions of each of the 34 strengths, visit http://bit.ly/JPStrengths.

Who Is This Book for?

Anyone who wants to make their work team better, or be a better team member, or be a better team leader, or be a part of a JoyPowered™ team. Enjoy!

Create Your Own Action Plan

Before you begin reading, please refer to Appendices A and B and bookmark them for easy access. Each time you feel inspired by an idea or story in this book, jot your insights down on either the insight (Appendix A) or action-planning (Appendix B) worksheet. Your notes will become the inspiration you need, from first steps to long-term strategy, in creating your own JoyPowered™ team!

Why Team Matters

"…it's about understanding what brings others joy and acknowledging that it is not always the same from one person to the next. Therefore, it's not that there is one simple answer on how to bring joy, but the individual answers are simple."

- JoDee Curtis, *JoyPowered ™: Intentionally Creating an Inspired Workspace.*[2]

Defining Team

Team. /tēm/. n. v.

> **Noun.** *A group of players forming one side in a competitive game or sport. Synonyms: group, squad, company, party, crew, troupe, band, side, lineup.*
>
> **Noun.** *A Group of people with a full set of complementary skills required to complete a task, job or project. Team members operate with a high degree of interdependence; share authority and responsibility for self-management; are accountable for the collective performance, and work toward a common goal and shared rewards.*

Verb. *Come together as a team to achieve a common goal. Synonyms: Join forces, collaborate, work together, unite, combine corporate, link, ally, associate.*

Noun. *A team becomes more than just a collection of people when a strong sense of mutual commitment creates synergy, thus generating performance greater than the sum of the performance of its individual members.*

The word team can be defined in many ways. I love that it is both a noun and a verb. To me, that truly describes the power of a team – it represents a "thing," but to survive, and definitely to thrive, a team must be action-oriented, a verb.

JODEE

What we really want to know is more than just the definition. In this book, we set out to determine what makes an excellent team – a high-performing, strengths-based team that truly finds joy in working together – what we call a JoyPowered™ team.

Let's dig deeper.

Whether we like to be part of a team or not, we find ourselves on teams throughout our lives.

Some people say they prefer to work independently versus on a team, but most of us recognize that being on teams at various times in our life journey enables us to function at our best. My life has been enriched and more successful because of the teams around me - it doesn't matter if I am the leader, a follower, or a teammate. I need teams to push me further, to stretch me, to encourage me, and to enhance my skills, but

joy**powered**

also to question me and to slow me down. For me, success in all aspects of my life is greater because of my ability to work in, build, lead, and contribute to teams. Let's explore some of these different types of teams.

Workspace Teams

For the purpose of this book, we are focused on **workspace teams**. I define the term "workspace," as the environment where you work. Your workspace might be the living room couch, the local Starbucks, a home office, a cubicle, your car, the corner office overlooking the city, or some combination of all of the above. Your team may be just you, as a solopreneur whose team is made up of the contractors, collaborators, and vendors who support you; you may be on a small team that is part of a large organization; or, in fact, you could be part of a team that is any size or shape. We believe this book will be helpful to anyone who strives to make his or her team JoyPowered™.

We chose not to write about volunteer teams or teams that might form temporarily for a particular project or purpose. Our focus is on-going business or mission-driven teams that have long term goals and plans, although team members may change occasionally for a variety of reasons. We also want to address one type of team that we are NOT including: family. We think you will enjoy *The JoyPowered™ Family,* which discusses one of the most important teams we are a part of – our family unit – but that is not the topic of this book.

It really bothers me when I hear work teams or entire organizations described as being "like a family." Who

am I to judge what that means? If people feel like their work team is a family, then so be it. But for me, there are some vast differences.

In an article on the Purple Ink blog, *Why Employees Are a Team, Not a Family*, Catherine Schmidt writes, "the term 'family' evokes a feeling of being valued, nurtured, and cared for – all good traits, so what's wrong with that?"[3] Comparing family and work, though, isn't always conducive to the best atmosphere for achieving goals. I had a conversation with a friend describing his father-in-law as a kind and generous man, but when it came to a family lake house they shared, my friend said, "he wants to run it like a business, not as a family home." There is a difference!

Work teams are trying to be successful, and that might be measured in terms of net income, sales, number of jobs created, or growth in clients and people served. In families, each person defines success differently. Families aren't necessarily working together to achieve a common accomplishment – there might be a goal to spend time together, to be loving, to show respect, to be faithful, but typically not one measured by dollars or metrics.

Organizations have an identity larger than the sum of its parts – their brand and culture. As work team members come and go, there is an impact on the team, as we will explore in chapter seven, but the company itself usually stays true to its mission, vision, and values. Families may have traditions, but a family is ever-changing, from marriages to births to deaths to divorces, and any one change can be big enough to forever alter the dynamic.

Most importantly, work teams can strategically select which players are added to fill a need or which players

joypowered

might not fit the needs of the team. There is no candidate selection process for families, as we usually don't get to pick our siblings, parents, and children. We may have beautiful, kind, and thoughtful people on a work team who would make great family members, but they might not have the skills, strengths, and/or drive to be successful on our work team.

Don't get me wrong, I love my family – my immediate and extended family – and I also love my Purple Ink team, but I do view them and treat them differently; and I want them to do the same with me.

Strengths-Based Teams

A strengths-based team, as defined by Gallup ®, is a group of imperfect but talented contributors who are valued for their strengths and who need one another to realize individual and team excellence.[4] Members of strengths-based teams are aware of each other's talent filters, and they understand how each person is inclined to think, act, and feel. This awareness helps the team navigate the issues that all teams encounter. They understand how the team can work best together to accomplish its goals and performance objectives. Gallup® research has shown that a team's direct path to growth and improvement begins with a primary investment in each person's greatest talents.

At Purple Ink, we describe ourselves as strengths-based. Are we perfect? No. Do we make mistakes? Of course. Do we always focus on our strengths? No. But we are intentional about knowing, appreciating, and combining not just our strengths, but also our skills - our

skills as business developers, service providers, writers, editors, planners, and goal-setters.

We constantly talk about our strengths, share how we are using them, and ask questions about others' strengths. We offer ongoing strengths coaching to each of our employees. We know it's important to be thoughtful and intentional to make ourselves and the team better. What I love best is that we understand how each person is inclined to think, act, and feel. This understanding helps the team navigate issues, projects, and feelings. We understand how our team can work best together to accomplish our goals and projects.

Our team isn't the only one that has benefited from focusing on strengths. Per Gallup® research:[5]

- Teams that focus on strengths every day have 12.5% greater productivity.

- Teams that receive strengths feedback have 8.9% greater profitability.

High-Performance Teams

Even when we have work-life integration, nice benefits, lots of team bonding, and find joy in our work, I suspect most of us are still looking for more. We want to be part of a successful, profitable, and high-performance team as well.

In *High Performance Habits*, Brendon Burchard describes a successful team as one that is "succeeding beyond standard norms consistently over the long term."[6] He defines high performers and high performing teams as:

- More successful than peers yet less stressed

- Enthused about challenges and more confident

- Healthier than their peers

- Happy

- Admired

- Reaching higher positions of success

- Working passionately regardless of traditional rewards

- Assertive for the right reasons

- Seeing and serving beyond their strengths.

- Uniquely productive

- Adaptive servant leaders

Until you hire them, though, how do you know who has this skill and who doesn't? How might you choose teammates who can consistently use their strengths over the long term? We can't just look at good grades, job experiences, or success in a single role. It's about understanding their values, their styles, and their strengths and how they interact.

JoyPowered™ Teams

In my first book, *JoyPowered™: Intentionally Creating an Inspired Workspace*,[2] I didn't set out to define the term *JoyPowered™*. Rather, I encouraged others to think about what that term might mean to them. For me personally, a JoyPowered™ workspace means:

- I look forward to starting and doing my work

- I have a positive influence on my clients and team members

- My clients and team members have a positive influence on me

- I consistently receive recognition that empowers me ("consistently" and "recognition" are defined by me in my own terms - enough for me and in ways I wish to be recognized)

- I can create opportunities to do what I do best more than 50% of my day

- My team members are using their strengths and finding their joy

- I think about what is right with teammates, clients, and prospects more than I think about what is wrong with them

- My team members and I are all able to learn and grow

- I am powered by faith and can express it as such

Some of my favorite definitions of JoyPowered™ provided by others on our team:

"I believe my work needs to help people or businesses get better, be better, or feel better. When I do that, I feel joy!" – Susan W.

"Having that frenetic energy that comes with feeling directed, impactful, confident, and productive…getting a lot done and doing it well." – Peggy H.

"A JoyPowered™ team trusts, communicates, and challenges each other while celebrating successes and learning from failure." – Laura N.

"A JoyPowered™ team is resilient, [and] all team members' points of view are valued, heard, and problem-solved together. This encourages creativity, productivity, and teamwork, where people love coming to work!" – Erin B.

"[A JoyPowered™ team is one] where each member is able to use their strengths and feels fulfilled in their role. They understand each other's strengths and how they can best be used to achieve a common goal or mission. Whether they're 'friends' or not, they care about each other as people, not just the work they do." – Emily M.

"A JoyPowered™ team is one that values the unique strengths and contributions of each team member, while getting its power from a commitment to a shared mission." – Caitlin A.

"Having a purpose for my days and looking forward to strength-driven, purposeful work that brings joy to myself and those I work with and for." – Liz Z.

"Working with a group of individuals who care about, trust, and love each other, share a common mission, celebrate each other's gifts, and consider the individual successes of teammates to be equally important as the success of the whole team." – Denise M.

Some of the key traits I described as being important to a JoyPowered™ workspace can also apply to a JoyPowered™ team; be intentional about:

1. Using your strengths.

2. Recognizing and appreciating. Follow the Platinum Rule: treat others as they wish to be treated. Find out how your team members wish to be recognized and appreciated, and then do it.

3. Encouraging constant creativity. Start by using your team's creativity to discover ways to be a more JoyPowered™ team.

4. Setting clear expectations. If you don't set them, ask for them. When we don't have expectations, we assume them (or someone else does).

5. Making the connection to the mission, purpose, or goals of the team.

6. Moving forward. Whether you are at the beginning or in the middle, keep moving or let quitting be the victory. Is it time to disband? Is it time to move someone off the team? (See chapter seven) Is it time to create a new team?

From the surveys I did for *JoyPowered™* as well as research on the subject using books, blogs, articles, and podcasts I've listened to on the subject, I believe everyone wants team members to:

- Be kind

- Acknowledge others

- Teach

- Celebrate

- Show appreciation

- Express gratitude

Creating a JoyPowered™ team does not have to be expensive or time-consuming, but it does have to be intentional. You can develop a JoyPowered™ team that will be more innovative and more profitable as you nurture more positive, healthier, happier employees who serve internal or external customers better and stay with your team longer.

The Purple Ink Team

Throughout the book, we will use our own team at Purple Ink in many examples. Currently, our team is made up of seven full-time and four part-time employees along with two regular contractors. Two work from different states than the rest of us, and all of us work from home at least some of the time (most of us work from home more often than not).

We catch some flak for not representing diversity because we are all educated Christian women. But we are also professionals, moms, daughters, grandmas, spouses, sisters, in-laws, educators, trainers, speakers, recruiters, consultants, writers, podcasters, and coaches. We come from a variety of educational institutions, including Indiana University, Purdue University, University of Evansville, DePauw University, University of Michigan, Anderson University, Butler University, and even St. Charles Borromeo Seminary in Philadelphia.

We hold a variety of credentials: Society for Human Resource Management – Senior Certified Professionals, Society for Human Resource Management – Certified Professionals , Professional in Human Resources®, Senior Professional in Human Resources®, a Certified Public Accountant, a Gallup® Certified Strength Coach, a Master of Arts, a Master of Public Administration, and two Certified Professional Résumé Writers. We majored or specialized in Psychology, Communications, Business, Accounting, Theology, French Literature, Sports Psychology, English, Spanish, Journalism, HR Management, and even Cosmetology. We have experience in manufacturing, healthcare, professional services, start-ups, education, churches, financial services, sports entertainment, insurance, technology, and non-profits. We also range from the ages of 23 to 65. Sounds like diversity to me!

Our Work

When it comes to identifying as a JoyPowered™ team, what you do is not as important as how you interact, but I will tell you what we do. Purple Ink is a human resources consulting firm based in Central Indiana. We work with clients in all industries, all sizes, and all over the United States. Sometimes our clients are small and don't have an internal HR team; sometimes they have thousands of employees with a hundred HR team members. Our mission is *inspiring JoyPowered™ work*. Our goal is to help both the individuals and the organizations be better.

We offer leadership training and development, team building, CliftonStrengths® and career coaching, talent acquisition services, a wide range of HR consulting

joypowered

services, and HR outsourcing, where we might fill a vacant HR role or supplement an organizational HR project for the short or long term. Our constant goal is to be flexible, positive, and creative in helping our clients create truly JoyPowered™ workspaces.

Building a Team

I take pride in having built a JoyPowered™ team at Purple Ink, yet I can't tell you I have always followed my own advice in recruiting, hiring, leading, and team building. I've made some hires that didn't last long and made two incredible hires who left our team. Our team has evolved a lot over the last nine years, but I could not be prouder of our people, our accomplishments, our innovations, and our clients.

I won't tell you I'm the best team leader, although many from the outside imagine that it would be "fun" to work with me. I have a reputation for being creative, positive, flexible, and not afraid to take risks. Past and current team members, though, will tell you that I have high expectations, hold people accountable, and talk a whole lot about achieving goals, goals, and more goals. We have off-site retreats, tickets to NBA games, and theatre tickets; we've had cooking competitions, a team party at a professional Ultimate frisbee game, and played TopGolf; but simultaneously, we each have accountability partners and billable hour goals, and consistently push each other to be better.

So, whether I built the team the "right" way or not, we are strengths-based, and we are JoyPowered™. We are also ever-evolving and changing – within our roles,

our services, our assignments, our clients, our use of technology, and our approaches.

How I Built My Team

I looked for people smarter than me, with different strengths and styles than mine and each other's, people who are more detailed than me (because I'm not detailed), people who value what we can offer (lots of flexibility but not all traditional benefits, independence but sometimes loneliness, work-life integration but high expectations), and people who want to be better by supporting each other.

I've tried very hard – but can also do more – to:

- Be kind
- Acknowledge others
- Teach
- Celebrate
- Show appreciation
- Express gratitude

But more importantly, I have intentionally hired people who are better than me at all of the above.

In *High Performance Habits*, Brendon Burchard asks,

"How do you drive the business yet step back enough to get all those people you so carefully selected to do their very best…getting scores or people acting in an aligned fashion so they achieve the goals of the organization, and understanding when to be a

cheerleader, inspiring and engaging others, and when to wield the hammer of accountability?"[6]

———

This is a constant challenge for me, as I believe it is for most leaders at Purple Ink and at any organization, but a good question to continually ask ourselves.

First Who, Then What

In one of my favorite books, *Good to Great* – an oldie but a goodie – Jim Collins asks the question, *"first who, then what?"[7]* This is a difficult concept, though. Don't we need to focus on *what* in order to determine the *who*? Do we create a vision (the *what*), then hire people who believe in it, or hire the right people (the *who*) to help us form the vision? In the book, Collins describes it as the importance of successful companies getting the right people on the bus, a metaphor for hiring and retraining employees who fit a company's culture. It is a concept that is relatively simple and makes perfect sense, yet somehow it is often overlooked, as too many leaders hire mostly for competency and technical skills.

Ahhhh, a concept that we as recruiters battle every day with our clients. We can teach skills, but not personalities, styles, or "culture fit." Yet, if we hire only for "culture fit," are we including diversity? There's some truth in all of it, right? The danger of hiring after the *what,* though, is a bigger risk, as we may hire people who think, talk, and act like we do and do not question our *what.* Hiring for the *what* can create a model where the leader creates helpers to follow his vision, and when the leader departs, the model fails. In looking back at teams I have built, there is one in particular that I felt at the

time was one of my most successful teams. We were productive, achieved high-level goals, and were JoyPowered™; yet when I left, the team did not succeed. It was not because I left, it was because I hired for the *what* and that went away.

In the YouTube video *How To Build A Winning Team - 5 Best Team Building Practices*, Robin Sharma lists five things the best entrepreneurs do to build a winning team:

1. **Appreciate them.** The number one reason you lose or gain people is whether they feel appreciated by a manager.

2. **Create a sense of belonging**. Make connections for people; every person should feel they belong to a special community.

3. **Help them grow**. Challenge them, develop them by giving them feedback, grow their talents.

4. **Celebrate process wins**. Don't just acknowledge wins at the end of the year, and celebrate the small things.

5. **Constantly evangelize your purpose**. Leaders of great companies are constantly sharing a clear concise vision for the future, one that their team falls in love with.[8]

These are not so different from my own list, but I especially like number five, constantly evangelizing your purpose. This helps keep people focused, on task, and committed to the goal.

We asked in a survey what qualities, skills, or strengths our respondents would look for on a JoyPowered™

team. These are some of their responses; do you agree?

> *"Supporting each other, willingness to all pitch in and get things done, listen[ing] to each other, recogniz[ing] and celebrat[ing] individual as well as team accomplishments."* – Jen H.

> *"...a positive team that faces challenges with a solutions-oriented approach. Work is always going to have stressors. It is all about how you approach those stressors."* – Leslie D.

> *"...people who love what they do. They are intrinsically motivated. There is Empathy and integrity. The leader does not have to command because the team members want to perform well and be successful. Everyone can be vulnerable and there is a high level of trust."* – Jamie F.

> *"A strong sense of leadership, not necessarily in one specific person, but the sense that the team is working toward a common goal."* – Nick S.

> *"The ability to share, listen, focus, accept others' ideas, recognize others' achievements, [and] be happy for others when they are successful."* – Mary Ellen G.

> *"Open communication, trust, sharing, laughter."* – Sherri C.

> *"Respect, independence, collaboration, follow through."* – Judi S.

> *"Intrinsic motivation, mutual trust, glass half full attitude, listening skills, respect for different*

perspectives, and the willingness to change/try new things." – Jessica S.

"Supportive, generous, forward thinking, goal oriented, focused, fun loving, open minded, enthusiastic and change accepting." – Mike D.

"Willingness to listen, enjoyment of each other, people doing what they do best, appreciating others' skills, and valuing difference." – Elli J.

Action Items

1. Write down how you define a JoyPowered™ team. Then ask yourself, are you on one? Why or why not? What are you doing to create one?

2. Which of your company values (whether formally written or informal) most helps you succeed as a team? Brainstorm actions you can incorporate to keep them alive on your team.

3. List the key traits of your team; do they match your JoyPowered™ answers in question number one? What are you doing about it?

Team Roles

"Individual commitment to a group effort: That is what makes a team work, a company work, a society work, a civilization work."

- Vince Lombardi

It Takes the Whole Team

Successful teams require a variety of skills, knowledge, and abilities. The best teams include individuals with unique strengths and talents, as well as diverse knowledge, experience, and expertise. JoyPowered™ teams are cooperative systems of talented members who complement each other and combine their skills and strengths to not only reach desired goals, but to stretch to a level far beyond the potential of any one single individual.

Teams form everywhere. We experience them in our homes, workplaces, political system, places of worship, doctors' offices, sports fields – even in the minutest colonies of our ecosystem. They are a natural part of the rhythm of life in almost all of its forms. We would do well to learn from both the big and the small.

joyPowered

Consider, for example, ants. Yes, ants. Ants are known for having teams that operate with efficiency. Each ant knows its role and carries it out with precision. The needs of the colony come first and every ant is a valuable part of the team's achievement of goals. They divide their labor instinctively on the basis of what makes sense to get the job done. From leader to crumb-carrier to nest-builder, the tasks an ant performs depend on its age, physical size, strength, etc.

It's a fact of nature that different team members are suited to perform different tasks. Roles on a sports team might be chosen based on physical size, strength, or agility. In the workplace, team roles are assigned and evolve according to many factors: experience, education, skills, strengths, expertise, ongoing training – the list is endless.

What's important in order for a team to be JoyPowered™ is to acknowledge that each role deserves consideration and respect for its value, as well as its impact on the final product. We respect equally the lowest to the highest paid, the humblest to the most prestigious position. It takes the whole team to produce the best results, provide the highest level of service, and best achieve the organization's goals.

"If we were all determined to play the first violin, we should never have an ensemble. Therefore, respect every musician in his proper place."

- Robert Schumann

The Team Leader

When we think of roles, it's natural to think first about the person in charge – a supervisor, manager, coach, parent, ant queen. Whatever label you use, it's the leader. The role of leader comes with both honor and responsibility.

Let's examine our own team at Purple Ink and our leader. JoDee Curtis started Purple Ink after working as a CPA and later as an HR Director in two well-respected accounting firms. She had the courage to go it alone, doing everything herself: finding clients, developing relationships, doing the work, and managing the books. As a result of her hard work and use of her various talents, her business grew, which required her to gradually grow her JoyPowered™ team.

Strong leaders are strategic. They intentionally hire with diverse yet specific talents, skills, strengths, and styles in mind. To make sure that she covered the full range of human resources services, JoDee deliberately hired people in five key areas: consulting, outsourcing, recruiting, training, and career coaching.

As she steered her strategic plan and grew her staff, JoDee utilized talent assessments such as Predictive Index® and, more importantly for this book, CliftonStrengths®. These tools provide ongoing insight into the preferred behaviors and strengths of each employee, as well as every team member's potential for growth and development. The Purple Ink team grew to thirteen with very little turnover. JoDee's approach to hiring continues to be intentional and organic. She focuses on the ability of each employee to add their

talents and gifts in a way that benefits the whole team and the mission and objectives of Purple Ink. Every member of the team feels valued and respected for the gifts she brings to the table.

Team Development and Strengths

Strong leaders develop their teams, which increases employee engagement and deepens the company's bench strength. This allows them to adapt and react to changes in the business climate. As our team grows, JoDee asks us for input about where we want to go and what we want to do to get there. Our team appreciates the generous opportunities for professional development. We learn and grow individually so we can contribute to the excellence of the team.

I worked on obtaining a Society for Human Resource Management (SHRM) certification and expressed interest in career coaching. As our roles shifted internally, I was offered the opportunity to take on career coaching, a task that engages my strengths and challenges me professionally. I have the strength of Adaptability. In addition to career consulting, I engage my Adaptability when I am outsourced at a client's office on short notice or take on a recruiting assignment. Having roles that allow us to develop and become specialists allows us to learn and grow, making our jobs challenging and more fun. It also makes good business sense.

Strong leaders also understand and accommodate the cycles and detours of life. A while ago, I was slated to work on-site with a client for a few months to help them while their HR Director was on leave. I met with them and was excited to begin the work. Circumstances

changed as I was called out of state to care for my mother. JoDee didn't hesitate to give me her blessing and calm my worries when my time off had to be extended. In true leadership fashion, she took the assignment off my plate and handled it, allowing me to focus on my family.

I truly appreciated JoDee's understanding and the ease with which she accommodated my situation. She had created a team with bench strength and could adapt to the situation. Our JoyPowered™ team was able to rally and find another HR Director to take on the role, which worked out for all parties. We are a strengths-based team. We are coached in our strengths, we regularly reinforce our strengths through in-house training, we know and appreciate our teammates' strengths, and we understand how our strengths work together to achieve success and excellence while accomplishing the Purple Ink mission.

A good leader asks her employees, "What do you want to achieve this year? What skills and expertise do you want to develop down the road? How can that help our business? How can I and your teammates help make that happen for you?". Regularly scheduled retreats, one-on-ones, and opportunities for goal setting allow for feedback and feedforward opportunities. Opportunities for goal setting occur at regular intervals and in the name of team development.

JoDee is a leader who imagined a team, has nurtured its growth, and continues to expand her leadership skills. She reads, studies, and implements many of the practices that strong leaders exhibit. Some of her favorite authors on leadership are Patrick Lencioni,

John Maxwell, and Marcus Buckingham. There are many great thought leaders who write about what it takes to coach or lead a successful team. If you have been given the gift of being able to lead others, I encourage you to fill your cup with knowledge and learn lessons from successful leaders.

Peer Leadership

Traditionally, we think of a team as having one leader and one or more additional contributors. But is that really accurate? Aren't we all leaders on some level, supervising, mentoring, and managing our line of business, clients, or projects? The responsibility of leadership on a JoyPowered™ team is actually shared, to some degree, by all.

In his book, *The Mentor Leader*, Coach Tony Dungy proposes this challenge: instead of asking, "How can I lead my company, my team, or my family to a higher level of success," we should be asking ourselves, "How do others around me flourish as a result of my leadership?"[9]

Dungy suggests seven rules of behavior for practicing leadership at any level. While all seven are insightful, I will comment on the seventh rule: "Complement your strengths with the strengths of others." Dungy advises us to remember that we were created for community. We were not created to do everything ourselves.

There are many roles on a team, and they vary from team to team. The team can be made of collective talents, or maybe some are superstars in their own right. I like to think that on our team, we are a collective talent and are all superstars in what we do. We take

pride in our own work and are proud of our work as a team. We all strive to make Purple Ink the go-to resource for HR solutions and JoyPowered™ workspaces.

Leadership is not all up to the team leader. Individual contributors impact others on the team as well. Think about how it feels to have a colleague compliment you privately or in front of others. Recently, I received an email from my colleague, Denise, about how she appreciated my feedback on some writing. It warmed my heart to read those kind words. I felt instantly valued and it reinforced that we are a team, each helping each other. Taking the time to thank, affirm, assist, train, encourage, or support your teammates, no matter what their job involves, demonstrates peer leadership. And it creates JoyPower.

Tony Dungy tells a story about Peyton Manning, the standout quarterback, who knew the team needed to work hard together to be successful. One summer, while Anthony Gonzalez was still finishing up his degree, Manning drove twice a week, almost three hours each way, to go over the playbook and throw the ball with the rookie, so he'd be up to speed on the plays. Manning did this quietly, with few people knowing about it. He was a leader on the field, a popular star, a celebrity in the community, and an individual on the team. He understood the importance of supporting each individual. He didn't delegate it to someone more junior. That's peer leadership in action.

Temporary Roles on a Team

When a member departs from a team, it's critical to figure out how best to fill that gap. Achievers and Activators may rush to fill that spot in order to check it off their lists and move on. While searching for the right person for that seat, a consultant may be a great alternative. While on-site, ask them to go beyond handling what comes across the desk. Take the time to learn their areas of expertise. Ask them to dig deep and point out areas where they think they can add value.

Purple Ink consultants are often brought in as temporary employees to fill the role of HR manager. In one such situation, we had a client with an adventure business that was specifically marketed to people in their twenties and thirties who travel. Company leadership wanted to have a fun and engaging culture that attracted employees in that same demographic, and they had big plans to grow with new sites opening across the country.

When our Purple Ink HR consultant read their offer letter template, she noticed that it mentioned in three different places how the prospective employee could be terminated. Employees were also instructed to sign a restrictive non-compete agreement and employee contract that wasn't necessary for the types of positions they were filling. Any joy brought on by the offer would be zapped upon its receipt.

Immediately we revamped the offer letter and created a more upbeat version that better represented the employer brand they were developing. This letter would appeal to candidates at any age who wanted to work for a company that celebrated travel, adventure, and a

positive culture. The legal department approved it, and it generated excitement in new hires instead of fear.

Later, this company decided to offer a great benefit to new hires: a free three-night vacation experience. While we supported the idea, it became clear that there was more to consider. Were employees being paid for the three-day vacation experience? Were they taxed if it was free? Did they have to go as a part of their training? What insurance was required?

As HR professionals, we get to infuse joy into the workplace, but occasionally have to suck the joy out of a great idea. This is a line we walk, but it's doable, and ultimately, our role is to figure out a way to make it work. And we do! With contributions from the whole team, the CEO, Field Managers, Finance, Legal, and HR, we were ultimately able to offer the vacation experience to employees with confidence that it was well thought out. This company embraced new ideas and was open to learning from a person in a temporary role on their team. Everyone was excited about the new offer letter and the innovative perk. It drove engagement and JoyPower with new hires and associates in the field.

Determining the Best Role for You

Sometimes we get thrown into roles, and sometimes we choose roles. Did you know that baby boomers have an average of twelve jobs from the age of eighteen?[10] I always thought that I was very stable and not a job hopper until I counted the different roles I held from the age of eighteen. It turns out that I had fifteen jobs! There's a reason we take all of those jobs, and one of the reasons is that we are trying to figure it all out. We

don't typically do a lot of self-assessment in our teens, and we aren't very in touch with our strengths, so we take a job because it looks cool or because our dad brought us an application.

In my case, my first job (at age ten) was cleaning my dad's office building. I'm not sure that my dad was thinking too much about my strengths, but it was a job. The next job was dropping a community paper door-to-door biweekly, then going back monthly and asking people if they'd like to pay for it. In retrospect, I probably used my strengths of WOO and Communication quite a bit in that job, but I dreaded when I had to collect. People wouldn't answer the door, some would tell me to quit throwing the paper on their step, and very few actually paid. It was deflating and sucked the joy out of me.

I won't take you through every job, but in time I became realistic about what my needs were. I loved babysitting, enjoyed sales contests at my job in the mall, felt professional in my job as a bank teller, and most importantly, I needed people to be the focus to feel JoyPowered™ in my work. There were jobs that came up later in life that I knew I could have gotten by saying the right thing in the interview. And maybe I was curious to try it, but by being in touch with my strengths, I am able to be realistic about what I do well and what is going to make me feel JoyPowered™.

To know what your role on the team is, you need to start with determining what types of roles are right for you. Begin by understanding your strengths. Whether it's from an assessment, feedback from others, or a result of your own deep reflection, discover what drives you.

Taking a walk down memory lane is also valuable. Write down every job you've ever had, even if it's a paper route or babysitting. Do you see any patterns with the types of jobs you took? Are they people-oriented or task-oriented? Do they require analytical skills or communication skills? Write down your memories of the responsibilities you had, what you liked, what you disliked. Think about what tasks you avoided or procrastinated on. In my newspaper example, I hated the collecting part because sometimes dogs would bark, and often people barked at me too! I got stomachaches, procrastinated, cried, and complained. Every sign was there that this was not the role for me.

Conversely, when I was a waitress at an Irish pub on my college campus, I loved going to work. I enjoyed talking with the customers; my coworkers were a ton of fun and I loved the music, the environment, and the thrill of counting my tips at the end of my shift. Try to detail exactly what aspects of certain jobs gave you stomachaches and what jobs got you excited. Often, we get energy from tasks that use our strengths and we feel drained by jobs that don't use our strengths. My waitressing shifts flew by, while the paper route seemed to take forever. Time flies when you are JoyPowered™, and that's what you want at work!

After you make your list, do some analysis of the roles and see what patterns are there. When and where were you most JoyPowered™? What were you doing? Who were you with? How can you use this information as you assess what roles you are the right fit for you?

As you reflect on your roles, consider some of Susan Cain's insights from her book, *Quiet: The Power of*

Introverts in a World That Can't Stop Talking.[11] Cain raises awareness about the difference between extroverts and introverts. Often extroverts command greater attention because they are louder and they ask for it. It's helpful to identify whether you are more introverted or extroverted and how that may or may not play into your career choice. It's a misconception to think that introverts are always quiet or that they can't speak in public or be leaders. Many introverts are powerful public speakers and even behavioral motivators. They may just not enjoy socializing with strangers at networking events. Get in touch with where you are on the extrovert-introvert scale and consider it as you assess your role.

Using External Assessments

We've been talking largely about self-assessments, but there are external assessments that can be hugely beneficial in determining your role. Ask your current colleagues, supervisors, friends, and others to share what they think your strengths are and perhaps what areas they feel don't really leverage your strengths. This can be tough, but the information from others can be priceless. If your team is able to use a 360° feedback assessment, you will get a 360° look at your performance, behaviors, and strengths by subordinates, peers, supervisors, and sometimes clients. It's invaluable to learn from all stakeholders in an anonymous format. Ask your coach or leader where they feel confident in your performance and where they worry, then ask why. For it to be helpful, you need their candor. Getting their perspective will be another piece of the puzzle.

joYpowered

Doing a formal career assessment such as the Strong Interest Inventory® can be useful in determining the type of career or role that may be a fit for you. The Strong Interest Inventory® measures your responses against a myriad of different jobs and shows the types of positions and activities that might fit your unique interests and personality. Ideally, you should choose jobs and roles that align with your interests. This is super helpful when you are deciding what type of job you want, but it won't necessarily translate into what role on the team you should play.

The CliftonStrengths® assessment, as we've already mentioned, provides valuable insight into your strengths. By knowing the strengths of individuals and plotting them out to see the strengths of the team, you can see into how best to deploy team talents. By being in touch with your own strengths and having knowledge of the strengths of your teammates, you can feel more confident raising your hand for certain assignments and passing on others. Since we are a strengths-based company, meaning we discuss, study, and intentionally focus on our strengths, we set goals that use our strengths and divide tasks strategically.

For example, there might be a job that requires many different skills, both interpersonal (relationship building) and analytical (think spreadsheet analysis). There are people who have both of these skill sets for sure; however, what if the person assigned to the task isn't strong in both aspects? What do we do then?

Purple Ink works with a client that had a phenomenal VP of Sales. This VP consistently brought in more business than her company had ever seen before.

When she was hired, she made a business case for having an administrative assistant. The assistant's salary, in the range of $45,000, was only a small portion of the revenue generated by the VP of Sales. They agreed to her terms, though having an assistant was not the norm for this company. Only the most senior level executives had administrative assistants, and even then, most of them didn't feel they needed one.

This type of sales was highly regulated and involved a great deal of paperwork and strict compliance with government laws. They were also subject to yearly audits. Sales boomed, management changed, and the administrative assistant came to be viewed as a luxury. They reasoned that they were catering to the VP's laziness and lack of follow-through on details.

The assistant's position was eliminated, and the VP of Sales began making mistakes. Her lack of follow-through on the paperwork increasingly became a problem. Disgruntled and disengaged, the VP of Sales quit. Company sales suffered greatly. What company leadership failed to realize is that to be a great sales manager requires certain strengths that didn't necessarily involve crossing the t's and dotting the i's. They could hire someone to do that part of the job, giving the VP greater space to do her job – making sales.

Sometimes we write job descriptions for the ideal team player, who we define as being everything to everyone. We need to step back and ask ourselves, what is critical for this role and how can we help this person best use their strengths? It's not that the sales manager was incapable of filling out the paperwork or crossing the t's and dotting the i's. She could do it, but it was draining

joYpowered

and an inefficient use of her time. The assistant enjoyed handling the details and did it quickly and accurately. Together, they made a great team.

The VP was positively JoyPowered™ when she was out wooing customers, making connections, and racking up sales. The administrative assistant was positively JoyPowered™ when she was dealing with things in the office and making sure that every detail was executed perfectly. The entire office reaped the benefits of the increased sales and attention to detail because there were fewer errors to fix. Sometimes, we need to think about whether the job description makes sense for the role.

Defining Your Role

When considering a job, typically you start by reviewing a job posting. Job postings should be fun, exciting, and challenging. The job posting is supposed to attract the best and brightest; it should be selling you on the merits of the position. Prior to accepting the job, ask if you can review the job description. This is an entirely different document and will often list every mundane task that could possibly fall under your purview.

Remember to ask for an explanation of such clauses as, "up to and including anything asked by management." Be inquisitive about aspects or requirements that you don't feel align with your ability to execute the main directives of the job. Recall our VP of Sales? If filing sales reports, crossing t's, and dotting i's doesn't seem like a fit, ask about how often you would perform these tasks or what technology the company

uses to assist with filing those reports. Know what you are getting into. You need clarity on what is expected.

Role clarity is important when you start your job, for both you and your supervisor. The VP of Sales was getting the message that sales were of the utmost importance, but when she was constantly harassed about paperwork, she had to refocus her energy on paperwork and not prospective clients. Consequently, sales dipped. You can't always have your cake and eat it too.

It's wise to agree on the job description and review it annually, or anytime a new employee is hired into that role. Make sure that it's still relevant and that the person feels they will be using their strengths. If not, is redirecting a task to another member of the team a possible solution? Maybe some rearranging would make several people more productive and JoyPowered™.

Communication is the key. Make sure to openly discuss what the needs of the organization and the team are. Realistically assess how your personal needs can be met within those conditions. Finding your role on a team is about understanding yourself and your teammates. Where can you best use your talents to help the team? If you are the quarterback and your skill is passing, who is your receiver and how can you best work together to capitalize on both talents? This is a fun puzzle to solve, and the more you communicate and work together, the more JoyPowered™ the team will become.

As you can see, there are many opportunities to discover your role on the team, whether it's receiving coaching from your leader or using assessments for self-discovery and team discovery. Discerning your role can be a process that opens your eyes to many

joypowered

possibilities where you can truly live in your strengths zone and bring your unique talents into their full potential. Whether you are in an office, on a sports field, or trudging up an anthill, you'll know you are in the right role. You and your team will be JoyPowered™.

Action Items

1. List your favorite job and your least favorite job. What is it about them that puts them in those categories? Think what, where, why, when, and how.

2. Define your role. When you are in a meeting or group project, what role do others look to you to take on? What roles do you tend to take on? Are those the roles that you want to do?

3. Think about your ability to lead. Is your strength leading people, projects, company initiatives, clients, or leading as a subject matter expert? Who looks to you as a leader? What are they seeing in you? What needs to be developed? Ask an employee, a peer, and your boss what you can work to develop.

Embracing Team Diversity

"Diversity: the art of thinking independently together."

- Malcolm Forbes

D iversity became a buzzword years ago. Today, diversity has its own buzzwords: microaggression and unconscious bias, to name a few. We'll get to those later. But long before it was a buzzword, people like Gandhi, Maya Angelou, Martin Luther King, Jr., and John F. Kennedy were talking about diversity.

When I speak to organizations on diversity and inclusion topics, race is almost always the first thing people ask about. It doesn't matter whether I'm in a room full of white men and women or if I see a great surface-level diversity in the audience, race is top of mind. Racial diversity is an important element in building diverse teams and continues to be a focus of division that exists today in our country, cities, and workplaces. But race inclusion isn't the only reason why I'm passionate about diversity.

joypowered

Today when people at work hear diversity, they think, "Oh no, we have to talk about diversity? Who got in trouble? Are we getting sued?" But once the awkward gets out into the room, we create a space where people are listening. Then our diversity conversations turn into dialogue that includes words like **heritage, opportunity, individuality, ability, value, thoughts,** and **experience.** These are the words that shape who we are, create our diversity experience, and drive my passion.

Diversity is Good for Business

What business today isn't looking for a smarter, more creative, and more productive team?

If diversity were easy, everyone would do it. And research shows that many diversity efforts are fruitless or even harmful to the workplace. So, what do we do?

As HR professionals, we see hiring managers continually hire versions of themselves for their departments. The "people like me" bias and building of homogenous teams is prevalent in many organizations. Research at the University of Michigan shows that hiring a specific type can actually lead to poor performance.[12] And diverse groups solve problems better than a homogenous team, even when that team has higher objective ability. A 2015 McKinsey report on 366 public companies that were ethnically and gender diverse performed significantly better than those that were not diverse.[13]

Why don't we all commit to diversity and inclusion? Well, other studies have shown that diversity can create discord that can make it hard to get things done.

Diversity is hard. Plain and simple. People are complicated. There is no single process, program, or magic bullet that works for everyone. We must train our managers and take the time to appreciate the hard work of inclusion.

That same McKinsey report found that those in the top quartile for ethnic and racial diversity in management were 35% more likely to have financial returns above their industry mean, and those in the top quartile for gender diversity were 15% more likely to have returns above the industry mean. So diverse teams are more profitable.

Diverse teams are also more creative. In *The Art of Innovation*, Tom Kelley describes the innovation process at Ideo, a global design and innovation company.[14] At the heart of their process is understanding that the moment of creativity arises when "multiple unique insights are combined to create something novel." Diversity! Any project efforts at Ideo start with their innovation team's exposure to diverse experiences. They accomplish this a number of ways: watching their customers, purposeful work with diverse team members, learning how different objects or materials work. This brings joy and sparks innovation used to inform creative thinking.

The Society for Human Resource Management has been studying diversity and its effects for many years. In addition to increased productivity and smarter teams, diverse teams also experience higher employee morale. They show five ways employee morale is boosted:

1. Individual validation

2. Productivity Increase

3. Creativity Increase

4. Community Connections

5. Employee Satisfaction[15]

At Purple Ink, we focus on employee morale a lot, both with our clients and among our team. We closely tie morale to joy. We believe boosting employee morale not only helps increase productivity, creativity, and community, but also the joy or satisfaction employees find in their roles and within their company. I've never worked on a team that brings such different perspectives, strengths and ideas, yet is so JoyPowered™ at the same time.

My Personal Story

Almost fifteen years ago, I had the opportunity to attend a two-day diversity training hosted by Quay Kester, PhD, CEO of Evoke Consulting. I was working for a disability agency, and the agenda did include disability topics. But the first morning started out with a discussion on race inequities, when Quay asked, "Why can't they just get over it?" This launched a feisty conversation.

We dove into our personal histories, centuries of oppression, and the challenges in the struggle for justice. I thought, "What have I gotten myself into? How am I going to deal with this stress for the next two days?" Women, men, black, white, people with and without disabilities, and the list goes on, talked about the challenges they face because of deeply rooted institutionalized systems which perpetuate oppression.

And while they represented groups of people in their collective struggle, influenced by history, what they really talked about was their individual experiences, where history plays out currently. We all want people to accept us for who we are. We need our individual thoughts and ideas to be recognized as contributing to the group, department, project, and company. We are all seeking the joy that stems from acceptance and respect.

It's not about getting over it, it's about getting into it. The stress I felt that morning was fear of the unknown. I didn't know the people around me, and I couldn't believe we were going so deep into a sensitive topic at 8 a.m.! But that's what we need to do at work, in our own teams. We don't truly know our co-workers. We have surface level conversations, we contribute enough to get a job done, and we go home.

Is that valuing diversity or creating inclusion? I've learned through my diversity journey that our workspace is the main place most of us encounter these opportunities for learning and growth. Unless you are the guy who walks out your door and thinks, "I'll go meet that neighbor today. He looks completely different from me; I'll start an awkward conversation about our differences." Let me know how that works for you!

Even in networking groups, we look like a middle school dance. Both men and women tend to gravitate toward people they know or who look like them and pretty much stay in our own corners. You have the greatest opportunity to learn about people who are different from you in your workplace. Since most of us spend more time with our work team than our actual family, take it as a challenge to get to know someone different.

Why? You have to know where someone's coming from to appreciate and understand an individual's contributions, let alone value them as a person. Surely, no one would say, "all the white guys want this," or, "all the women will choose that," or, "we need this for the people with disabilities." Oh wait…we do that all the time. In HR, we are usually understaffed and overcommitted. We need to move fast, find efficiencies, and help the organization meet its strategic objectives through people. Consequently, we lump people together and make decisions for the collective group. We don't know individual preferences, tastes, or choices people in that group would actually make, but we would if we asked.

People don't want to talk about diversity, because a lot of people don't think they are diverse. As an HR professional who does a lot of recruitment, I'm sometimes asked for diverse candidates for consideration. What is that? A biracial millennial? A man in a wheelchair? A woman wearing a hijab? One person can't be "diverse!" When we think of our team, we must shift our definition of diversity to a group of people working together in a setting bringing a variety of individual identities of self. Another way of describing diversity is "people thinking independently together!"

Defining Team Diversity

"How can you govern a country which has 246 varieties of cheese?"

- Charles de Gaulle

Team diversity is defined as differences between individual members of a team that can exist on various dimensions like age, nationality, religious background, functional background, sexual orientation, and political preferences, among others.

Different types of diversity include demographic, personality, and functional diversity, and have positive and negative effects on team outcomes. Diversity can impact performance, team member satisfaction, or the innovative capacity of a team. As the old saying goes, the two things you don't talk about at work are religion and politics!

Now, I'm not suggesting you condone politicking or place a focus on religion in your workplace, but how can you know someone at work if you don't know their basic values and belief systems? In the long term, lack of this knowledge affects performance, stifles innovation, or at a minimum, squelches team member satisfaction. Have you ever thought of hosting a religious tolerance dialogue during lunchtime as a learning opportunity? Would you allow space for people who want to discuss political issues or inequities they see in your workplace?

When we close ourselves and our offices to these types of discussions entirely, diversity is stifled. Lack of diversity leads to misunderstandings, inappropriate comments, and isolation, where your workplace could be vulnerable to discrimination and ultimately harassment. The U.S. Equal Employment Opportunity Commission (EEOC) keeps statistics on discrimination, both total charges as well as charges by type of discrimination.

A review of charge statistics over the last ten years, not taking into consideration charges filed with local or state

joYpowered

Fair Employment Practices Agencies, shows what a lack of diversity does. In 2017, there were 84,254 total charges filed. Race, Sex, and Retaliation are generally the three types of discrimination with the most filings each year. In 2017, of the 84,254, there were 28,528 individual filings for Race, 25,528 for Sex, and 41,097 for Retaliation.[16]

These numbers tell us we've got work to do! Nearly 100,000 charges were reported. We not only have a liability as an employer to provide equal opportunity, we have a responsibility to prevent workplace harassment. This starts with policies in the workplace that are enforced. Undoubtedly, Fox News had an anti-harassment policy when Bill O'Reilly settled his $32 million sexual harassment case. Surely Mercy General Hospital in Sacramento had some type of education for all employees when a federal jury awarded physician assistant Ani Chopourian $168 million after she endured two years of a sexually hostile work environment. She had complained numerous times to no avail.

We have to go beyond policy, online tutorials, and a process for resolving discrimination complaints. Now don't misunderstand, these are the foundation! We must have a safe workplace first where everyone understands how to play nice in the sandbox. What we're driving at here is true inclusion, where diversity is celebrated and differences are in demand; a place that's JoyPowered™! So, where do we start?

Minimizing Bias

I am biased. And trust me, that's difficult to say. But even harder to hear, maybe, because you are too. We all are, in fact. Bias is an inclination, a tendency, a leaning one way that can cause us to stereotype or have an attitude towards something. Our biases can come from our parents. Before you write me off as another perturbed millennial, bias is ingrained in us.

In *Political Tribes*, Yale Professor Amy Chua notes that we are hardwired to be suspicious of others.[17] Our brains tell us to trust the familiar. As a kid, each time my babysitter showed up, I knew my mom (the familiar) was going to leave, so I cried. This wasn't learned, it was automatic. And now, my daughter does the same to me. She doesn't like the unfamiliar. She wants things the same, NOT different. It's a basic instinct that has protected us and helped us survive for thousands of years. But today, since most of us aren't fighting off bears, we have time for more than a fight-or-flight response and more resources at our disposal than any time in history. There's no excuse for our bias, once discovered in our consciousness, to remain.

What is unconscious bias? "Learned stereotypes that are automatic, unintentional, deeply ingrained, universal, and able to influence behavior," says Mike Noon, Professor of Human Resource Management at Queen Mary University of London.[18] You take these small acts of bias or prejudice and they become so regular you don't notice them, but they take a large toll on the person in the marginalized group. That's microaggression.

joYpowered

Microaggression is a catchall term, "used for brief and commonplace daily verbal, behavioral, or environmental indignities, whether intentional or unintentional, that communicate hostile, derogatory, or negative prejudicial slights and insults toward any group."[19] Let's say a group of women of color walk into a restaurant. They're seated at a less desirable table than the white group coming in. And they don't get the same service as the white group.

You may think this doesn't happen today, but I personally have been part of a predominantly black work group, and I experienced this microaggression as part of the group. And when it happens in your workplace, it creates a hostile climate. Being the victim of microaggressions can hurt your self-esteem, and over time, your health. No one wants to work in a place like that. But unfortunately, this is far more the norm than the exception. And our friends in minority cultures have been enduring it for years.

Gender-based stereotype expert Saundra Schrock is a friend of Purple Ink, and on The JoyPowered™ Workspace Podcast with JoDee Curtis and Susan White, she talks about managing bias through mindfulness.[20]

Saundra says we must be aware that every human being has a filter through which they see the world. When we realize there is a filter, we can learn to think differently. Ask yourself, "What lens am I looking at the situation through?" Mindfulness is a miracle to see people for *who they are*. But Saundra realized it isn't a miracle, but a practice. The practice of "functional mindfulness" is taking everyday activities and turning

them into mind training for the present moment. Applied to our teams, we should embrace all employees in organizational conversations on a number of levels. This means intentionally including those in different departments, different levels in the organization, and a "fresh eyes" perspective, which means getting uncomfortable. When we embrace the discomfort, that's how we learn.

If you want to better understand your bias from the comfort of your own home, try the implicit association test (IAT). Harvard University researchers started Project Implicit® back in 1988. The IAT measures attitudes and beliefs that people may be unwilling or unable to report. You can take a demo test on categories like age, race, country, gender, weight, skin-tone, disability, sexuality, and the list goes on. You may be surprised with your results!

Once we acknowledge our bias, we can start to understand how to minimize it, retrain our brains, and ultimately advocate and advance those in our spheres who are different. In Dr. Sandra Upton's *A Black Woman's Advice to White Professionals*, she focuses on Acknowledge, Advocate, and Advance.

Dr. Upton explains that it's important to **acknowledge** that even though everyone has biases and may experience prejudice, people of color are the primary recipients of racism. **Acknowledging** that working across cultures is challenging is a crucial step.

She also suggests that if you're in a leadership position, you should attempt to exert your influence over the employee lifecycle to **advocate** for a diverse organization and inclusive culture.

Finally, Dr. Upton says that we can **advance** our cultural intelligence through acknowledging and advocating.[21]

At Purple Ink, we're thankful for this advice, as we consider candidates and colleagues in their job search almost daily. We strive to ask ourselves about Upton's areas of focus. Are we acknowledging our bias when we realize it? Are we advocating for diversity and inclusion? Are we advancing ourselves and those around us as a result of our advocacy?

Becoming JoyPowered™ Through Diversity

Purple Ink is currently working with a client that is being intentional in diversity and inclusion efforts. The President said in our first meeting that a one-time training or event wouldn't have the lasting impact he wanted for his workforce. What we heard him say was that he was seeking JoyPower!

Together we laid out a diversity and inclusion plan for the calendar year, starting with Diversity, Inclusion, and Hidden Bias training for all employees. Next, we invited interested employees to participate in a focus group to gauge areas of interest and to gain employee buy-in. We discovered a reality that is common in many workplaces: employees felt great about the diversity in their organization overall, but inclusion wasn't happening equally across the board.

Our client established quarterly lunch 'n learn sessions to focus on the areas of diversity most important to all employees, starting with bias and privilege. Leaders in

the organization were provided further education and training on the topic. Together they decided to read a book about diversity, *What If? Short Stories to Spark Diversity Dialogue* by Steve Robbins, holding monthly discussion meetings about each chapter. They are also paired with a coach, who meets with them individually throughout the year to help them in areas like diversity recruiting, employee relations, and how to establish or enhance their own JoyPower through diversity and inclusion in their departments.

Management is now seeking ongoing employee feedback and monitoring progress through regular pulse surveys that are already fostering open communication. In just three short months, our client has already seen an increase in awareness and action around diversity. Employees have started to recognize bias in customer service practices and are identifying opportunities to improve procedures that reflect greater commitment to diversity and inclusion.

Increasing Diversity on Your Team

In December 2018, Fortune published a list of the 100 Best Workplaces for Diversity. The list focuses on the experiences of women, people of color, the LGBTQ community, employees who are Baby Boomers or older, and people who have disabilities. When I think of a "great place to work," my mind doesn't automatically think hospitality or retail. But surprisingly, topping the list are Hilton, Comcast NBC Universal, and Publix Supermarkets, Inc. So, what is Hilton doing to be a great place to work, driving diversity and inclusion?

According to Fortune, Hilton's performance is "extraordinary across all demographics, including

ethnic and racial identity, gender, age, disability status, and sexual orientation."[22] Hilton has great representation in each category, and those employees also say the company is a great place to work. Of Hilton's 55,000+ U.S. employees, 69% are racial or ethnic minorities, 53% are women, 5% identify as LGBTQ, and 4% have a disability.

Hilton's Vice president of Global Diversity and Inclusion, Jon Muñoz, comments,

---

"Diversity is embedded in our DNA. It's important for us to reflect the communities where we live and work. We're in the people business, so it's important for us to be responsive to our guests, our team members, and our communities."

Companies who understand diversity know that representing the local community is key. When people work and live in community, diversity and inclusion flourish. Hilton focuses on Team Member Resource Groups, or TMRGs. Of the fifty chapters, TMRGs at Hilton include those for African Americans, the LGBTQ community, Latinos, women, veterans, people with disabilities, and others. Muñoz leads the people with disabilities chapter, and while not disabled himself, prides himself on bringing a focus on ability. In addition to providing education and a sense of belonging to employees, the TMRGs provide opportunity for professional growth and feedback on company experiences, and ensure voices across the company are being heard.

At first glance, our Purple Ink team looks pretty homogenous. If you look at our website, we are all women. We joke about this, because we actually have men on our team, but they are collaborators, referrers, and supporters to this feminine powered machine! Maybe we just haven't found the right guy yet, but I digress.

As previously mentioned, our ages span five decades and we've had a myriad of different experiences. Looking at our strengths, we cover all 34, and the differences in creativity, flexibility, and positivity (our core values) never cease to amaze me. From high school grads to master's degrees, our team's educational background is diverse, and this Butler Bulldog tries her hardest to be inclusive of her IU and Purdue teammates.

The variety of our work experience is what I think makes us so valuable to our clients. Whether we're working with a manufacturing company, healthcare client, accounting and finance firm, or church, we have Purple Inksters whose backgrounds include those specialties. And it allows us to serve our clients because of our diversity of experience.

Looking at other companies, we asked over 200 people, "How is your workplace diverse?" We found that people identify diversity in the following areas in their organizations:

JoyPowered Survey: How Is Your Workplace Diverse?

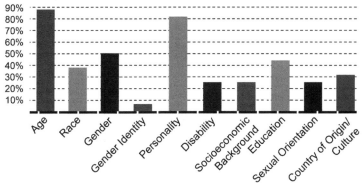

We then asked, "Is there a difference between diversity and inclusion?" Here's what our respondents said:

> *"Diversity is about differences in people: cultural, ethnicity, beliefs, gender, etc. Inclusion is about creating a supportive, encouraging, open environment."* – Anonymous

> *"Diversity is simply having a diverse workforce, while inclusion is about making everyone in your workforce feel welcome and a part of the same team."* – Ashley B.

> *"Diversity is being aware of the differences that separate us, but inclusion is about learning, celebrating, and mak[ing] choices that honor those differences."* – Amanda H.

> *"Diversity is having differences; inclusion is accepting those differences."* – Andrea S.

> *"Diversity is being diverse, but inclusion is making everyone feel included and welcomed."* – Anonymous

"To me, diversity means hav[ing] people of many different types of backgrounds, and inclusion means everyone is a part of the team regardless of backgrounds." – Jolaine H.

"Diversity is about the people and who they are. Inclusion is about them being able to be who they are openly in their workplace without fear of ridicule or reprisal. Inclusion is feeling accepted with your differences and not having to leave who you are at the office front door." – Anonymous

"Diversity means many things, like different backgrounds, and inclusion is to get everyone on the field at the same time." – Jack P.

"Diversity equals acknowledgement of all human differences. Inclusion requires action...proactive behaviors that help others feel valued, respected, and that they belong." – Toni N.

"Inclusion is about inviting diverse people to be involved and provid[ing] them with equal opportunities to contribute their diverse thoughts, ideas and perspectives. Diversity is bringing diverse people together to be involved. The key to D & I is involving diverse people and creating an environment and culture where equality and diversity is welcomed and valued." – Britt G.

"Diversity can be merely the presence of multiple people from varying backgrounds, races, religions, cultures, identities, etc. Inclusion is a healthy representation of members from each of

those groups in leadership and decision-making." – Anonymous

"Diversity is being invited to the party; inclusion is being asked to dance."

- Verna Myers

Building a Diverse Workplace

Now that you've seen the value of diversity and inclusion in your workplace, how do you create a diverse culture? At the 2018 HR Indiana Conference, Jenn Lim, the Co-founder and CEO of Delivering Happiness, responded to that question with…"you don't." Your culture is who you are, it's your DNA. If your culture is inclusive, then the diversity will come. "Strategy is the *thinking*, brand is the *talking*, and culture is the *doing*," Jenn said. What are you doing to drive inclusion so your workplace will be more diverse?

In the Wall Street Journal's *Building a Workplace Culture* guide, some of their tips to help increase workplace diversity include:

- Develop a hiring strategy to make your workforce resemble the community you operate in.

- Talk to local community organizations to help find candidates.

- Ask existing employees for referrals.

- Provide diversity training in your workplace.[23]

Diversity in your workplace will be a reflection of you, so know what your needs are. Do your employees match the community you serve or the demographic you want to serve? Reach out to community organizations, local colleges and universities, and churches to help with your hiring strategy. Ask your employees to refer great people they know and reward them for doing so. If people are JoyPowered™ in their jobs, they tell their friends and family, who then want to work there too. And keep diversity and inclusion top of mind by training your employees, annually at a minimum. From your diversity training, affinity groups or resource groups like those at Hilton may be a natural next step. Start with the diversity you have and grow it from there. Mentoring programs across the levels of your organization are another way to foster growth, build relationships, and encourage inclusion.

The most important decisions in building a diverse workplace are who to hire and who to promote. Rocío Lorenzo says the answers to these questions send the most powerful message in ANY organization. In her TED talk, *How Diversity Makes Teams More Innovative*, Lorenzo said, "when you hire and promote for diversity, they understand that in embracing diverse talent, we are increasing opportunity for everyone."[24] According to her study of more than 170 companies, in organizations with the highest innovation and success, at least 20% of leadership roles were held by women. We can no longer tout the one woman on our board, or the HR Director who is the only female on the leadership team. Innovation revenue rises when more women are at the decision-making level in the organization.

Another valuable TED talk is Rebeca Hwang's *The Power of Diversity Within Yourself*.[25] Rebeca describes

joypowered

herself as a Japanese-looking Korean who speaks with a Spanish accent (Argentinian to be exact). And instead of trying to be any one of those things, because she never fit in when she pigeonholed herself into one aspect, she embraced "Rebeca-nese." When she stopped looking for commonalities and embraced the different versions of herself, she found her joy! From Rebeca, we learn to cultivate the diversity within us, not just around us.

Following My Passion

I was raised by example to reach out and help others whenever and however I can. That, combined with my natural curiosity about others who are different than me, has led me to a variety of positions and situations my entire life where not only have I been witness to microaggressions, I have sometimes been the "minority" who experienced them.

In my first job out of college, I worked in the disability community, helping individuals become gainfully employed. At my next employer, a small community hospital, I started their first Diversity Discussion Series. Next, I served medically underserved populations partnering with healthcare institutions to train health professionals and serve local communities. As an HR Director, I increased female workforce numbers in the male-dominated professional auto racing industry, hiring the first women in roles like Race Engineer and Mechanic. Many people, myself included, don't realize the diversity journey they are on. My entire career, I've been following my passion of helping others and pursuing my joy.

A couple years ago, I started attending the 3DG: Diversity, Discipleship, Discussion Group at my church. This group is in the real business of diversity— leading lives that are inclusive through building relationships based on Christ. "Biblical Unity in Diversity." The call of the church. I have neighbors who are of different races, ages, and disabilities, but do I know them? This is what I'm called to do. Not advocate, train people, or even bring awareness, but to KNOW people.

This fall, I had the amazing opportunity to experience a Civil Rights trip with many members of the 3DG and leadership from College Park Church. This bus trip ventured to the deep south, opening my eyes to things I'd studied, but never knew. We visited heart-wrenching places like the 16th Street Baptist Church, the Lynching Memorial, Civil Rights Museum, and Emmett Till Memorial. I learned about the crushing systemic connection between lynchings and keeping entire groups living in fear for their lives for decades after slavery was abolished. I learned how mass incarceration is the new slavery, why people today can't get over it (and shouldn't), and just how little I really knew the people sitting right next to me on any given Sunday.

The most influential time of our trip was on the bus; listening, lamenting, and asking questions of my brothers and sisters, who so patiently answered the same questions they've answered all their lives. I can now say I actually know people who are different than me at my church, not because I know their name, but because I know their story. That is diversity in teams.

Last year, my husband and I adopted a biracial son. My life and the story of my family has been forever

strengthened ever since this decision, not to mention truly JoyPowered™! This blessing reinforced my belief that we, as leaders, need to ignite the drive in our team members to reach out and understand each other's uniqueness, heritage, and stories. A team who does this will be stronger because of it.

"Our ability to reach unity in diversity will be the beauty and the test of our civilization."

- Mahatma Ghandi

Action Items

1. Celebrate the diversity currently present in your team through inclusion and diversity training, after hours socials with "get to know you" questions, and acknowledging holidays outside the mainstream that are fun for all.

2. Establish a recruitment plan that attracts diverse individuals. Use apps like Textio or Unitive to check your job ads for stereotypes. Consider translating your application and any job-related information online to languages that reflect your customer/client base.

3. Brainstorm how increasing diversity on your team will help you be more JoyPowered™.

Why Teams Succeed

According to the Oxford Living Dictionary, success is defined as the accomplishment of an aim or purpose and/or the attainment of popularity or profit. A synonym of the words "aim" or "purpose" is the word goal, something I believe all successful teams should focus on. My definition of success is achieving my goals and accomplishing my tasks in a timely manner. Success or failure are simple to diagnose, but the path that leads a team there can be more difficult to define. The path to success can be analyzed by looking closely at a team's leader, their communication style, their focus on goals, and their commitment to the organization.

"When the leader decides to put the safety and lives of the people in the organization first, remarkable things happen"

- Simon Sinek[26]

---

joypowered

Great Teams Have Great Leaders

Leadership and development

Great leaders put an emphasis on leadership and development because they know investing in their employees is an investment in the company. This alludes to Richard Branson's famous question:

CFO: What happens if we invest in developing our people and they leave?

CEO: What happens if we don't and they stay?

Workplace studies have shown that companies absolutely cannot afford the costs of poor leadership. According to Ron Carucci, a Harvard Business Review contributor, developing employees creates a more competitive workforce, increased employee retention, and higher employee engagement.[27]

You might think of leadership development as continuing education through tuition reimbursement and expensive training programs and certifications. In fact, US companies spent over $90 billion dollars on training and development activities in 2017.[27] These are the initiatives that make CFOs panic – and many companies truly cannot offer this kind of contribution. Although Richard Branson would tell them that they can't afford not to offer it, leadership and development does not begin and end there.

A mentorship program can be developed for free. Match up less experienced employees with more seasoned

workers to create an environment of mutual learning. This can be as structured or as non-structured as you would like, but it is recommended that these individuals meet at least a few times a year.

Here at Purple Ink, we meet with our "accountability partner" once a month to check in on our personal and workplace goals, project accomplishments, and how we can best support each other. We recognize that our team creates an abundance of knowledge when we combine our experiences. This knowledge is too valuable not to share, and we are so fortunate to have each other to not only bounce ideas off of, but to challenge and continue to experience new things together.

There is an abundance of reasons why employee development should be important to an organization, the first being that employee development attracts young talent. A study at Brookings stated that millennials will make up 75% of the workforce by 2025.[28] These young workers are going to need innovative strategies and leadership skills to be successful, and they will be attracted to the companies that recognize this need. Only some of this can be learned at work, while much must be learned by additional training and opportunities to learn from other leaders in the field.

Secondly, employers that develop their employees experience loyalty. Employees that are learning continuously and recognize that their workplace wants to invest in their development will be more likely to stay at the organization longer, as well as create a bigger impact on the organization. Third, training and development breeds a competitive advantage for an

organization. The invaluable information that employees learn by being developed comes right back to help the organization succeed and outperform the competition. Investing in employees is not only an investment in your team's people, but in the organization's success.

Purple Ink is committed to developing its employees. As stated in chapter one, we have many individuals who hold Human Resource Management certifications. In addition, we are putting two more team members through a SHRM – Certified Professional study program, and another team member is getting certified as a Strong Interest Inventory® interpreter. This allows us to be known as trusted experts in the HR community. We have a culture that values learning at all stages of life, we talk about CliftonStrengths® almost daily, and we encourage each other to always set and reach personal and professional goals.

Feedforward

Great leaders give consistent and conversational feedback. Purple Ink refers to this process as feedforward performance management. Our definition of feedforward is information that is shared to help us move forward, not just a focus on the past. Great leaders practice feedforward because they recognize that employee development is an ongoing value.

Annual performance reviews are not frequent enough. Employees need regular feedforward direction. If leaders only evaluate performance once a year, there is a great likelihood that they will rate that person's performance based upon the last six weeks of work, not

the entire fifty-two weeks the employees have put in. This is a product of the recency effect, a popular topic of study in social psychology.

The recency effect occurs when more recent information is better remembered and receives greater weight in forming judgement than does earlier-presented information.[29] However, if regular informal conversations discussing employee performance are added, employees will have a better idea of what is expected, and issues will be resolved much faster.

Employees should always know where they stand in terms of performance. A Forbes study on employee performance stated that a mere 29% of employees said they *always* know whether their performance is where it should be.[30] This is not productive, because if employees aren't being told that they are doing something below expectations, they may not know that a change is needed.

Forbes contributor Mark Murphy indicates that when there are more frequent performance conversations happening, employee goals can be addressed in greater depth, leading projects to advance more quickly with a higher success rate.

Are we saying ditch the annual performance review? Absolutely not. Annual reviews are important for an overall evaluation of the year. However, informal ones should be happening all the time. The annual review should be clear and simple, and it can usually be short. All criteria should relate to employee performance. It is also advisable to include professional development in the conversation. Former CEO of General Electric Jack Welch, who was also Fortune's Manager of the Century in 1997, encourages leaders to use professional

joypowered

development as a reward for great performance in his book *Winning.*[31, 32]

At Purple Ink, our leaders do a great job of frequently discussing employee performance, while also having formal mid-year and annual performance check-ins. Our founder, JoDee, takes every opportunity to share performance information with me, teach me, and build confidence in my work. She gives very frequent feedback, often within the day, on any project or situation that comes her way. This approach allows projects to constantly progress and evolve. In a training JoDee attended many years ago, Mary Mavis said, "How dare you have information about someone that could help them be better and not share that with them?" This question affects how JoDee leads her team to this day.

Employee Focus

Great leaders are just as focused on their employees as they are on their customers. In order to create mutually beneficial relationships with employees, a leader must know them personally, value their opinion, and give them the respect that they desire. To achieve accountability, engagement, and results, team members should be managed on an individual basis. This means taking the time to dissect what makes employees work effectively – what gives them energy and what does not. Every employee is going to have different needs, wants, and career goals. A great start to learning more about your employees is to have them take an assessment. Purple Ink recommends the CliftonStrengths® assessment or the Predictive Index® assessment.

Once leaders know what motivates employees, they will begin to see them excel at the tasks that drive them. Positively influence each team member's psyche daily, not only through leading by example, but by being optimistic and upbeat about business. An enthusiasm for what one is doing is contagious, and every team member will want to be involved. They will spend much of their free time talking about their company to family, friends, and even the guy in the grocery line.

For example, I once had a job that would look pretty darn boring to others. I stood behind a half-moon shaped counter for eight hours straight and scanned the same hundred fitness center membership cards day after day. Once a day, I had the added displeasure of scrubbing down the locker room, tanning beds, and gym equipment with harmful chemicals – cleaning everything from weight machines to dirty toilets. However, to me, this job was anything but boring, because I had the most motivating manager!

Not only did she care about me personally, respecting my personal life and school schedule, but she knew how to get inside my head and make me care. She knew I was a natural leader, so she often gave me the job of motivating other employees to do their jobs better. She knew I loved to talk to new people, so she would sign me up to give any and every tour of the gym. She also knew what tasks did not give me energy, and she simply gave those tasks to others who were a better fit. She did this with every employee I worked with and we all were incredibly happy with our positions.

My manager at the gym has received two promotions since my resignation and most of my coworkers have since moved on, but I still try to stop by and see how the

gym is doing when I am in town. If I become a manager in the future, I plan to follow my past manager's leadership style, because it is excellent for engaging and retaining employees.

"Individually, we are one drop. Together, we are an ocean."

- Ryunosuke Satoro

Great Teams Communicate Consistently and Openly

Have you ever worked with a team member on whom you could fully rely? Even better, what about a team of people that you could trust? I have a feeling if I were to propose these questions to a group of professionals, many would be raising their hands and nodding, as most employees truly want to be great team members. As a recent business school graduate, I have experienced this type of group a few times and find it to be the most successful work environment. Let's explore some strategies that set the stage for good team communication.

Trust and Cooperation

First, trust and cooperation must be at the core of the team. There are many ways to foster trust, but the simplest yet most effective is just getting to know one another. In the age of technology and workplace flexibility, which I will cover later, it becomes very easy

to develop "good enough" results without knowing those you work alongside.

While researching JoyPowered™ teams for this book, we asked a group of business professionals, "If you consider your team to be successful, what is your secret? If not, why?" One respondent, Tracy B., nailed it when it comes to the topic of trust: *"Trust is HUGE!! We all trust each other to do the right thing, to do our jobs, to keep things confidential."*

To be truly in sync with your teammates, know what drives them. What are their work styles and communication preferences? For example, I was in a training a few weeks ago where we were discussing workplace recognition. Recognizing employee accomplishments is something we do a lot at Purple Ink - we love celebrating each other's workplace and life victories. Our leader, JoDee Curtis, was sharing this with a group, and everyone seemed to agree that it was positive until one person piped up: "I really don't appreciate being recognized that way. It makes me uncomfortable." The dynamic changed, not necessarily to something negative, but more of a discussion on how people like to be recognized.

In chapter one, JoDee mentioned the Platinum Rule: treat others how they wish to be treated. It is so important to find out how individual teammates would like to be recognized for their efforts. Some may eat up the public praise, while others may prefer a private "good job" in an email or one-one-one.

Once there is a better understanding of one's teammates, working together becomes not only easier, but much more productive. Colleagues will start to combine each other's talents and strengths. At Purple

Ink, we use CliftonStrengths® as a basis for learning how each teammate works best. We consider knowing and recognizing each other's strengths a large contributor to our company's success. There are many different tools for finding out more about how to work better with a team. The key is finding the one that works best for your group.

Radical Candor

Once a team has a strong understanding of its people and their strengths, candor becomes effective rather than living out its stigma of negativity. Merriam-Webster's definition of candor is "unreserved, honest, or sincere expression." Jack Welch attributes much of his success as a leader to candor. He states in his book *Winning,* "We gave it to each other straight, and each of us was better for it." The conversations that come out of being candid with one another are rich in ideas.[32]

During my junior year of college, I was involved in a semester-long project with an assigned work team. Forty percent of our class grade revolved around teamwork, and most of our assignments were a group effort. We met twice a week and the group's electronic communication was constant. Although my team was highly successful, earning one of the highest grades in the class for our final project, the semester was incredibly challenging, because this was the first time I was introduced to radical candor.

My group was full of diverse personalities, but we were all very high-achieving students. We questioned each other's approaches and ideas constantly, we challenged one another on almost every decision

made, and we were often made uncomfortable due to the candid conversations. I felt uncomfortable because I was not used to my ideas being challenged, and I don't think several of my group members were either. I have to say, I was relieved when the semester was over, but appreciated the experience for the radical candor it produced.

I think back on the experience often in my professional life. How successful would we have been if we did not mull over every assignment? What mistakes would we have made if there was not a large analysis and multiple highly opinionated approaches? I certainly do not think we would have been as successful or learned as much as we did that semester, and I attribute much of that to the candor that occurred. I still communicate with several of my group members on occasion, and we all agree that the semester helped us grow as not only learners, but individuals.

Alternatively, in my last semester of college, I was a participant in a work team that ultimately did not succeed. Our team was assigned a semester-long business simulation, and we made weekly decisions about each department. There were several individuals on our team who immediately assumed they were the hypothetical CEO and their decisions would trump everyone else's. There were others on the team who did not care and simply did nothing. The individuals left in the middle were driven crazy by both kinds of teammates but refrained from saying a word about it.

Jack Welch describes this experience in *Winning*. "Most people don't speak their minds because it's simply easier not to."[32] There are many reasons why people don't communicate candidly. They may think it will come

across as rude, or that there will be negative consequences, that it will threaten their status with the team, etc. Not speaking candidly when it is needed can cause mistakes. Mistakes bore serious consequences with our group. The unauthorized chiefs were often wrong, but no one wanted to challenge them, so our whole team suffered as a result.

Our team dynamic was a disaster and our long, intense meetings were insufferable. It is not productive, fair, or realistic to contribute to a team with sub-par performers. At the end of the semester, the chiefs, the non-confrontational folks, and the slackers all received an average grade on the project – the ultimate consequence of work team dysfunction. We all paid the same price, despite the variations in our performance.

Great Teams Focus on Results

Workplace Flexibility

A 2015 study by the Society of Human Resource Management shows that workplace flexibility with a goal-centered focus breeds larger results than the traditional 8-to-5 workday in a boss-fearing culture. Of the HR professionals surveyed, 67% stated that employee productivity had increased with a flexible workforce and 59% saw an overall increase in work quality.[33] In a Purple Ink blog called *4 Ways To Make Your Workplace More Flexible,* Emily Miller explained that workplace flexibility reduces absenteeism and turnover, while adding to engagement and productivity.[34] Our modern workforce is being taken over by technological advances and the millennials that embrace them – and the work never stops. Professional

work is performed around the clock and often does not get done at the office. This shift in work life creates a shift in personal lives.

The topic of work-life integration has always sparked my interest. As a millennial and a recent college graduate, my hobbies are just as important to me as my career. Outside of work, I love to craft candles, read for pleasure, jog to reduce stress, and am pretty glued to most shows on Netflix. I was very interested in how other professionals rated work-life balance, and to be honest, I was blown away at how far work-life integration has come. Eighty percent of our survey respondents rated their work-life balance a seven or above out of ten. I was less surprised, but also very pleased, to hear the answers to the question, "How does this rating motivate you?"

"It is important to know that I have the flexibility to meet my family commitments even though my job is demanding." -Leslie D.

"It keeps me from changing jobs!" – Anonymous

"It is crazy important to me; I work a LOT of hours, but having the ability to volunteer, work when I want, etc., is of most importance to me." – Anonymous

"Knowing I have a great work-life balance makes me enjoy going in to work, knowing that if life gets in the way, I can take care of life and not feel guilty". – Judi S.

> *"Work well. Play well. And don't worry when the two overlap at times"* – Christine B.
>
> *"I don't think I could work somewhere that I didn't score this at least a seven."* – Terri S.

Others are conscious of the fact that their work-life balance could be improved. These answers are just as important as the ones above, because the individuals acknowledge the fact that they are lagging in work-life integration and recognize their need to improve.

> *"[It motivates me] to continue to work on getting that balance where I want it to be."* – Mike D.
>
> *"It makes me want to do a better job at balance."* – Tracy B.
>
> *"It tells me I still need some work on the life part of the equation."* – Jolaine H.
>
> *"I'm always looking for ways to improve my work-life balance, but struggle to find ways to keep myself on track."* – Nick S.

Results Only Work Environment

Some workplaces are adopting a "Results Only Work Environment" as a creative approach to helping employees achieve greater work-life integration. Daniel Pink, author of the bestselling book *Drive,* defines this as simply having to get one's work done.[35] How employees do it, when they do it, where they do it, and whom they do it with are up to them. It is the ultimate form of autonomy in the workplace. Pink has studied many workplaces that implement this type of environment – with some employees coming in as early

as eight in the morning for a meeting and others strolling in past noon with no explanations needed. As long as the individuals are meeting their goals, there will be no consequences. Goals are exactly what makes this type of work culture possible. Goals must be understood, accepted, and measurable to work in this environment.

I have experienced this type of culture firsthand at Purple Ink. Our firm believes that professional and personal life integration is essential for success. We are just about as flexible as any workplace you can find. In fact, we won a When Work Works Award from the Society of Human Resource Management in 2018 for our innovative and flexible workplace practices. Although we do have an office, every employee has the option to work remotely, using tools such as Slack, Trello, and Zoom to stay connected.

Additionally, our employees do not have a set schedule. Employees can work their agreed-upon number of hours at the times that work best for them and their clients. Purple Ink is extremely life- and client-focused. For some employees, that means having the flexibility to raise their children, for others it means having time to volunteer, and several employees simply like to spend a lot of time on their hobbies. This flexibility allows our team members to be available for their clients at times that would best serve an organization's needs. Our employees ensure that the expectations are set in advance and the objectives are clear, and they plan their schedules around what works best for those we serve.

Workplace productivity is measured for our team by tracking goal accomplishment, having clear expectations and deadlines, and holding each other

accountable. These are just some of the reasons why we continue to have a positive, engaged culture.

Great Teams Are Committed to the Mission and Vision

Do you know your company's mission? How about its vision? Do you believe in these things for your company and do they motivate you? The Business Dictionary's definition of a mission statement is "a written declaration of an organization's core purpose and focus that normally remains unchanged over time."

Consider the mission statements of a few well-known companies:[36]

- "To improve its customers' financial lives so profoundly, they couldn't imagine going back to the old way." – Intuit

- "To accelerate the world's transition to sustainable energy." – Tesla

- "To bring inspiration and innovation to every athlete* in the world. *If you have a body, you are an athlete." -Nike

- "To organize the world's information and make it universally accessible and useful." – Google

- "Inspiring JoyPowered™ work" – Purple Ink LLC

Do you think the mission statements accurately capture the continuing purpose of the companies they represent? They are inspiring. The Tesla mission statement made me want to go take a test drive. The Nike statement, "To bring inspiration and innovation to

every athlete* in the world. *If you have a body, you are an athlete," almost had me driving to the mall for my next pair of running shorts. Mission statements like these motivate people, and I am sure they get the employees excited to achieve great things. How does your company's mission statement add up? Does it motivate your team to do great work?

Purple Ink's mission statement, "Inspiring JoyPowered™ Work," permeates our culture. It impacts everything we do, whether it's recruiting, training, consulting, career coaching, or administrative work. The idea of consciously leveraging joy into my workday is something that truly keeps me going, and I would imagine my team members feel the same way. We see the impact of bringing JoyPowered™ workspace ideas to other businesses, and the results are truly astounding.

This topic came up in answers to our question, "If you consider your team to be successful, what is your secret? If not, why?"

> *"Everyone understands the vision and mission and is given the latitude and flexibility to get there using their personal mix of hard work, dedication, ingenuity, and smarts. Members of the team support one another and back one another up."* – Tela E.

> *"My team is full of smart, talented people who do especially well when they understand the organizational vision...the North Star to which we are moving. We could be more successful if that vision were clearer...without its clarity it can feel like we are just spinning our wheels without any traction."* – Jessica S.

I love Jessica's unique definition of vision, being "the North Star to which we are moving." That is exactly what a vision statement should be designed to do – move a company closer to their organizational goals. Mission statements are about the core of the business, while vision statements are all about the future. Your entire team should be able to recite the company vision statement without question or thought. Why? Because if you have a good one, it is a clear guide for choosing current and future action. It ensures that the direction your team takes is successful and smart for the business.

Once again, I will bring up one of my all-time favorite CEOs, Jack Welch. The man is a legend. He believes that your team should not only be able to understand and implement the vision statement, but they should play a part in creating it. If employees are involved in the vision creation process, they will do more than understand it, they will truly believe in it and carry it out.

Action Items:

1. Write down three things your leader does that helps make your team successful. Thank him or her for doing these things using the Platinum Rule, mentioned in this chapter.

2. Write down one or two positive things that you know about each of the co-workers you work with most of the time. This can be a strength, a work style, or a fun fact. Brainstorm how these traits relate to yours and how you can use them for increased productivity.

3. Take note of your team's workspace flexibility. Reflect on how this flexibility leads you toward or away from accomplishing your goals.

4. Review your organization's mission and vision statements. Brainstorm ways that these statements can motivate and drive you forward and write your favorite down somewhere that you can see it while you work.

joypowered

Why Teams Fail

"Working together does not mean you are a team. Striving to do great work together and caring about each other in the process means you are a team."

- Jon Gordon

If you don't care about or challenge your team, will it fail? YES! There is a high probability that it will. And if it fails, where is the blame placed, or where did it start? If you want to create a JoyPowered™ team or challenge your team to remain JoyPowered™, it is critical to heed any signs of failure. It is also up to the team to initiate changes toward the positive when recovering from failure.

Let's start with the definition of failure. Failure can be described as lack of success, the neglect or omission of expected or required action, the action or state of not functioning. We begin to see the reasons why teams fail right there in the definition of failure. Often, teams are created without a clear expectation of the outcome required. Without a clear definition of an actionable goal, teams will fail time and time again.

Teams are complex, dynamic systems that face many challenges. In fact, study after study shows that 60% of teams fail to reach their potential. Each person on a team has a role and individual strengths that propel them ahead to smash their goals. Again, that is if the goals are clearly defined and each member on the team feels sincere trust and loyalty in each other.

In 2015, Forbes contributor Jeff Boss wrote about three reasons why teams fail. He claimed that these are not the only three reasons, but they seemed spot on to me.[37]

No Opportunity to Build Trust

Boss proposes that opportunities to build trust are missed. Without these opportunities to build trust, teams will fail. In other words, teams fail due to lack of trust. You have to build trust and it takes time, patience, and vulnerability along the way. Boss further explains that trust can be broken down into two components: character and competence. First, is it safe to trust the person to be competent in his or her job; and second, do they have a positive intent and good will in doing so? You have to have both parts to grow your trust in a person. If you don't, then trust is lost, or never gained, and your team fails. Continuous and constant interaction creates trust. Boss explains that ultimately, if you want to build trust amongst a team, they must interact. He suggests taking work breaks at the same time, eating together, and simply spending time together to build trust (for more on trust, see chapter six).

joypowered

Throughout this book, we have inserted quotes or ideas from individuals that shared feelings about their teams with us. An example from Nick S. that demonstrates the importance of constant interaction: *"My team struggles to stay connected. We have strong goals and leaders, but we often have difficulty focusing on a common goal and establishing a plan to accomplish it."*

At Purple Ink, we have a connected team that sets goals each year to continue to find ways to keep our team on track and together. Purple Ink has team members who work at clients' locations, some who work from a central office, and some who work from home. Because we work in various locations, it's easy to be disconnected, and as our team grew there were some feelings of detachment. We intentionally set goals that force opportunities to connect as a solution to those feelings of detachment. Being a connected team is an important goal at Purple Ink.

We honestly do not believe we can have a JoyPowered™ workspace if we have members feeling stressed about our team, so we never want to lose sight of the mission. We have sampled several video conferencing systems to see which one works best for our remote workers, as well as for our clients. Recently, we implemented Slack as a communication channel among the team. Regardless of whether a team member is at the office, working from home, or working remotely at a client location, we can still be connected.

We also try to take this goal on personally. For example, every time I go to the office, I try to take a walk or quick lunch with another teammate. One of my connection goals is to include as many team members in these

activities as possible. From experience, I can definitely say that small gestures of inclusion work to build trust and connectedness.

Favoring Individuals Over the Team

Boss also rightfully indicates concern when incentives favor individuals over the team. If you consider a sales team rewarded for new business, you get the picture. It is very hard to challenge a team to increase sales, reward them individually, and expect the team be more cohesive. The individual competition can get fierce, and without a leader that either addresses the greedy teammate or gets rid of the individual, the team will be put at risk to fail.

At Purple Ink, we challenge each team member to be an advocate for growing our business. Our leader has explored a few reward systems for individuals sealing deals with new clients. We always come back and confirm that it is our entire team that plays into whether the clients are pleased, and we are rewarded with repeat business. If Purple Ink team members were only worried about the clients that they personally brought in (because of their commission earned), we would not be growing and succeeding. Each member must be passionate about building relationships with our clients and ensuring that we deliver on our promise.

No Open Discussion About the Team

Lastly, Boss concludes that teams fail when there is no open discussion about the team. This includes good and bad discussions about teammates. Every individual on a team should know their strengths (whether this be through CliftonStrengths® or not) and weaknesses. In a

joypowered

JoyPowered™ workspace you should not only embrace and share your strengths with the team, but also your weaknesses. Being vulnerable and open about any areas of work where you need help, passing along the details to someone who specializes in the weeds, or just sharing your fears will build trust. This trust will build a successful team instead of a team that fails.

I love the details of a project, tracking the progress and numbers along the way. Peggy, our Ideation teammate, admittedly tells us that she'd rather not get into the numbers; she is up front building relationships and coaching our clients. Even if this means we need to communicate more as a team to keep a project running smoothly, we know our strengths and that it's okay to keep Peggy out of the weeds. She doesn't need to know every detail behind the scenes. Creating ongoing communication with your boss and teammates will set the right tone and as issues arise in your projects at work, you will be in the habit of discussing them and better at identifying problems early on.

Emily Miller, Purple Ink's talented Manager of Marketing, wrote a blog titled *The Power of Failure*.[38] Emily's great advice, first and foremost, is "Don't wallow. Move forward and take action to fix it and you'll recover just fine." Emily explained that often in business, we fail because the expectations we set for ourselves are too high, and often ridiculous. Once we realize a goal is unattainable, we must move on quickly from failure to become successful. Emily reminds us to focus on the good and not spend much time on weaknesses. What will really bring joy to our workspaces (and our lives) is keeping the focus not on how we are failing, but on what we are doing well.

Among our Purple Ink team, we have several teammates that enjoy the details, working on employee handbooks and tedious HR Assessments. We also have other teammates that pass politely when they are offered these opportunities. Admitting an area is not in your wheelhouse is half the battle. Why would we want to assign the wrong person to a project only to have to spend more time on it? Additional time can add up, and if the strongest person on handbooks passed a handbook project to someone inexperienced, more time and frustration could lead to a project failure. On the other hand, we challenge our teammates to work on new projects and understand that there is a learning curve. But if someone realizes the new skill isn't a strength and they are not adding value to the project, we identify it, accept it, and move on.

"If failure isn't an option, then neither is success."

- Seth Godin

At the close of her blog, Emily asked readers to consider whether they're being too careful and avoiding risk, and if so, whether they're doing anything they're excited about. There is a lot to think about in that question, and many times, playing it safe can be the riskiest decision you make.

joypowered

Lack of Trust

"Teamwork begins by building trust. And the only way to do that is to overcome our need for invulnerability."

– Patrick Lencioni

I would be remiss if I wrote a chapter on why teams fail and did not include some insight from Patrick Lencioni. The fable he creates in his best seller, *The Five Dysfunctions of a Team*, is powerful.[39] A new CEO is faced with uniting a truly dysfunctional team. Lencioni details a model that helps the CEO explain to the team how to overcome hurdles. Through the fable, he is able to build a cohesive team by acknowledging the imperfections of the team and individuals. Lencioni defined his model as a triangle, and I'll explain it from bottom to top.

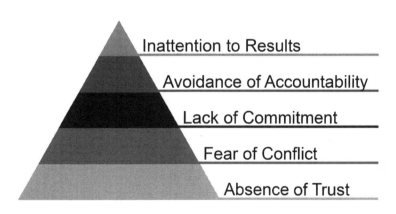

Absence of Trust

Obviously, you can see that trust is the underlying theme here! Lencioni states:

"Great teams do not hold back from one another – They are unafraid to air their dirty laundry. They admit their mistakes, their weaknesses, and their concerns without fear of reprisal. In the context of building a team, trust is the confidence among team members that their peers' intentions are good, and that there is no reason to be protective or careful around the group. Teammates must get comfortable being vulnerable with one another."

Fear of Conflict

Many teams I have been a part of have unfortunately created what is called "Artificial Harmony." Some of the team members might say that their leader does not allow them to form opinions. They believe that if they do not agree or go along with what has been decided as a solution to a problem, they will be ostracized or never given a promotion. This dysfunction goes hand in hand with lack of trust. If you do not trust your team, your willingness to challenge or question a team member is low. Often, people do not even think sharing an opinion is worth their time.

joXpowered

Lack of Commitment

How do you get your entire team to buy in to an idea or project? To maximize clarity and success, you must have commitment. If a project is not set with clear objectives and assignments, commitment will decline as ambiguity leads to a lack of buy-in. Purple Ink made the mistake in the past to assume that everyone enjoys getting together on a Saturday morning to run or walk a race for a good cause. Usually one member on our team is truly committed to the organization sponsoring the race. We've had very poor turnout, with only a handful of Purple Inksters supporting the event.

But we've learned that usually, it's not that no one wants to support the event, it's just that we all have other commitments and Saturday mornings can be the busiest! We've failed at supporting some of these events at the level we wished we could, so instead of throwing in the towel, we now look ahead and plan the year out. We notify everyone well in advance of these activities and only commit if we can get a good showing at the event. We are learning, but not afraid to try new events and activities just because they haven't been successful in the past.

Avoidance of Accountability

This can be a byproduct of accepting low standards. The blame can easily be placed on the manager, CEO, or project leader. There can be an unwillingness of team members to call their peers out on performance or behaviors that might hurt the team. All of these dysfunctions intertwine. If you don't trust your team or are afraid of conflict, you will not be comfortable

addressing issues. As time goes on, the team begins to accept this low bar, and performance drops.

This avoidance of accountability can quickly drain a team. A pitfall we see frequently with our clients is an inability to address issues in a timely manner. If a team isn't performing, the manager should immediately be identifying the problem or the individual at the root of the problem. Purple Ink's leader, JoDee Curtis, shared her experience in a blog called *How to Know When It's Time to Let Go*.[40] When an organization decides to fire someone, it doesn't have to mean failure for the individual or for the company. No one needs to stay in a job that isn't working. If an individual decides to leave an organization, they should not think that they failed the organization. Many times, it is not a good fit and both the organization and the individual realize that. JoDee recommends we use these situations as an opportunity to grow, move on, and celebrate.

If you find yourself struggling with your team or a specific individual, ask yourself these two questions posed by Jim Collins in the book *Good to Great*.[7]

1. Would you hire this person again?

2. Would you feel terribly disappointed or relieved if they came to tell you they were leaving to pursue an exciting opportunity?

If you can confirm that you would not hire them again or you would not be disappointed if they decided to leave, then you need to move forward in having the discussion about letting them go. A lot of times, the effect a poorly performing team member has on the team as a whole is overlooked. In her blog, JoDee advises that you should not be afraid of or avoid terminating someone.

Move forward, and you may very well be preventing future failure for your entire team. See chapter seven for more tips on letting team members go.

Inattention to Results

The goal of any team is to conquer problems that need to be solved. Regardless of how you get there, the celebration as a team should be at the conclusion of the project, whether big or small. Lencioni explains that individual status and ego can directly impact the team's success. Team members can seek out individual recognition and attention at the expense of results. All of Lencioni's dysfunctions go directly to the heart of why teams fail. A team member with an ego is going to crash the team at an alarming rate.

Ego

———

"It is amazing what you can accomplish if you do not care who gets the credit."

– Harry Truman

———

Anytime I hear the word ego now, I immediately think of Cy Wakeman. Cy is a drama researcher, international leadership speaker, and consultant. She has authored several books, the most recent of which is *No Ego: How Leaders Can Cut the Cost of Workplace Drama, End Entitlement, and Drive Big Results.*[41] Cy brings to the forefront that individuals are operating out of ego at work, which breeds drama. Cy insists that the time

wasted on drama costs companies millions of dollars, and she is on a mission to reinvent leadership thinking.

———

"Your circumstances are not the reason you can't succeed; they are the core reality in which you must succeed."

– Cy Wakeman

———

What a powerful statement, and true in every way! In *No Ego*, Cy hits the nail on the head as to why teams fail or cannot move forward. When she was a young leader of a high functioning team, Cy was asked to move her team several times in the span of just one year. The first couple of moves her team did well, kept their positive attitudes, and resumed work quickly. The third and fourth moves came with headaches, and when they were asked for a fifth time to move due to construction, her team was in revolt. She tried to stay upbeat and positive with her team, but she felt the same way, asking why they should suffer like this.

She marched to the CEO's office, and before she could speak with him, her mentor asked her, "Why is your team suffering?". Cy explained that it was inconvenient to move, it was unfair, and they weren't able to work efficiently with all the interruptions. Her mentor asked again, "But why is your team suffering?". A lightbulb went off with Cy, and she realized they weren't suffering because they were moving, they were suffering because they refused to adapt. They hadn't grown their ability to work in different ways and be mobile. The source of the pain was coming from the resistance to doing what was required for the business.

Cy went back to her team and told them that the next time they were called to move, they'd be willing and ready. Playing victim to circumstances will never allow you to get out of the suffering. If you turn to verbal suffering (venting), it only continues to show your lack of flexibility instead of a focus on how to move forward.

Cy provides numerous examples that created *aha* moments for me, especially when thinking back on work teams that I have been a part of. Working with individuals that only look out for themselves or want upper management to notice their contributions can be taxing. Both Lencioni and Wakeman agree. Leaders must rein in this behavior quickly. If individuals are not willing to collaborate, communicate, listen, and move toward a goal, it might be time to address whether they are meant for your team.

Letting Failure Define You

Mike Bensi is the founder of Bensi & Company, a consulting and coaching firm focused on creating healthier ways to work for organizations and leaders. Bensi's book, *The Success of Failure*, helps companies utilize their culture as a powerful differentiator and competitive advantage to help their business grow.[42]

According to Bensi, most people let failures define who they are rather than learning from mistakes and turning failures into lessons. The first step in creating success from failure is to stop "head-trash" and other useless thoughts. Bensi encourages people to take back ownership in life when it's been given to others and see empathy as a method to climb back up.

These concepts carry over to work. Think back on a time when you or a company needed to hire a new team member. Did the people responsible for hiring take the time to stop and consider the candidate they needed? And, even more importantly, did they take the time to plan how the new team member would be integrated into the team? We often see companies simply looking for immediate relief and training later. They end up replacing the replacement because they didn't take ownership and acknowledge the true need, do the hard work to identify the best fit, and nail down their onboarding process. Bensi explains if companies spent more time developing people, answering questions, and listening, less turnover and better cultures would be created.

Bensi strongly stands behind the concept that a great leader must pass out encouragement and celebrate their team members. He explains that even if a sports team wins ugly, they will celebrate the win in the locker room and then start correcting the mistakes. How often do we find ourselves focusing on the negative or what made us not win? Pushing pause, stepping back, and acknowledging the win allows us to support a positive culture. Whether it be a personal or corporate win, celebrate often. Simply focusing on a small win can change the tone of the team and push toward a big win – a great start in turning failure into success!

At Purple Ink, we'd like to think that we don't fail often. With each client we meet, we propose on a specific project and clearly set expectations. We also know we are human, and at times we might need to circle back to the client if the project leads to other priority areas. We are not afraid to admit it if we aren't equipped to tackle a project. We have numerous partners we reach

joypowered

out to for support. Each time we start a new project, we look back on similar projects and evaluate what worked or did not work. We are continually trying to ensure our process is as efficient and positive as possible. If we do fail, we share the experience, learn from it, and move on.

Each year at Purple Ink, we create annual goals, both personally and professionally. When I was hired three years ago, this was a new concept for me and definitely a challenge to get started. It truly opened my eyes to understand that goal-setting is important to keep us moving forward. Sometimes we fail, and that is okay. I feel that Mike Bensi would agree with our goal-setting approach.

Last year we were tasked with determining how we were going to celebrate our goals once accomplished. I will admit it was hard to set guidelines on how I would celebrate reaching a goal and to be honest, I might not have always celebrated. I know I need to work on this, but I have also realized that sometimes I do not reach my goals. I had one goal in particular that I never really started because when I set the goal, we were proposing on a specific project that needed additional system support. We never got the project or had the need to evaluate the systems. I might have failed on completing a goal, but I don't regret adding it to my list. The process of goal-setting positions us to move forward through a process all year, experiencing both achievements and failures.

Bensi shared similar insights in a blog we posted on the Purple Ink website, *A Leader's Response to Failure*.[43] Bensi shared that companies should be creating a culture where employees learn from mistakes, and

where failure and constructive feedback are part of the journey in learning and growing as leaders and as individuals. He suggests creating experiments or stretch assignments to test new ideas and assist in predicting future obstacles. It's critical to take the time out *after* a project to do what many organizations call "post-mortems"; determine how it went, what needs to be changed next time, and whether this is an area where you need to devote more time.

Bensi focuses on open communication, knowing it's okay to share when something has failed. Admitting defeat will only help others grow. Asking for feedback is a no-brainer. You must be vulnerable and ask, "What's one thing I can do better, or how can we (as a team) make this work better next time?" Lastly, to create success out of failure, Bensi notes that you need to prioritize learning. Managers must give feedback and allow staff to learn and seek educational opportunities to continually challenge the team.

Lack of Respect, Loyalty, and Communication

I have mentioned several authors who have focused their careers on determining why teams fail and how we can identify issues and make changes to be successful. All of their expertise includes ways to guide teams to conquer big tasks as a team, and yet the underlying message is that for a team to be successful there must be respect for all members. Also, it is acceptable to fail, but it's how you climb out of failure that means the most. Being able to work with a team that truly respects each other is what drives me every day and brings JOY to my life. In chapter one, JoDee told us how she built her

team, and the fundamentals of respect and loyalty were key.

"In teamwork, silence isn't golden, it's deadly."

- Mark Sanborn

For a team to function successfully, there must be open channels of communication. It is a sign that there's something chronically wrong with a team when members do not feel like they can voice concerns, express disagreements, or offer recommendations.

In 2017, Purple Ink received a call from the President of a large construction company asking for assistance in recruiting for a Controller position. The President was extremely fearful that she was about to lose her entire finance team. In our initial recruiting strategy assessment, she shared that the Controller had decided to retire early. The company was caught off guard and not prepared for the sudden departure. Within a few days, they promoted the company's Staff Accountant into the role.

Fast forward three months, and they were reaching out to Purple Ink. The leadership team realized the Staff Accountant was promoted prematurely. The individual did not have the knowledge, technical skills, or management experience to succeed in the role. The unfortunate part was that they had not yet shared their thoughts with this individual. They decided to seek outside assistance to fill the role first (confidentially) and then they would discuss next steps with that individual

and the team. When we started the search, they did not think they would be able to retain the former Staff Accountant as the relationship appeared severely damaged and they knew his loyalty and trust in the management team had diminished.

Purple Ink worked swiftly to fill the position and uncovered additional critical details about the finance team along the way. The Staff Accountant had gone silent, most likely fearful that he'd lose his job. He was working sixty hours a week and still could not get ahead of the demands of the Controller position. He lacked the ability to direct his team and was losing their trust rapidly. The leadership team was not communicating to each other until Purple Ink was able to sit them all down together to assess the potential candidates. After the three finalists were interviewed, we met for an additional two hours to lay out what the finance team needed to look like and how to build that team.

Through our JoyPowered™ approach, we recognized that the Staff Accountant was amazing at his former role before his promotion. We acknowledged his bookkeeping strengths and realized the company could not lose his experience. The leadership team had to be open and honest about the needed roles. In just three months, the department had lost its ability to work effectively as a team because of the lack of communication and trust in the roles.

Fortunately, we were able to select an experienced construction Controller to fill the role. Along with his accounting skills, he possessed managerial experience and sound leadership practices. The company was able to retain the Staff Accountant and by communicating honestly with him, they mended the relationship. Not

joy powered

only was the Staff Accountant happy to stay, he preferred his previous role to the duties of the Controller. The entire team continues to run smoothly and efficiently with the right people in the right places, with open lines of communication, and working with team members they can trust.

Why did this team fail? What if from day one, the leadership team had the time to get the right people in place? What if the Staff Accountant had set his ego aside, come forward, and admitted he was overwhelmed?

Well, they would have saved time and potentially saved the individual and the finance team from "failure." Yet by making these mistakes, they learned the importance of planning and open communication. They won't make that same mistake again.

Looking back, the President admits she should have had a succession plan in place, and she recognizes now that approaching staff with honesty, transparency, and open communication will in turn build trust and continued loyalty. She now knows what to look for in her staff, which will set them up for success instead of failure. At Purple Ink, we continually strive to educate our clients about what signs to look for in failure and how learning from those situations will move them forward.

Warning Signs

A 2016 Forbes article set out *14 Warning Signs That Your Team Is Nearing Dysfunction*.[44] We suggest this list as an examination of the health of your team. Being vigilant about these symptoms will assist you in

preventing failure. If failure is already rearing its ugly head, then perhaps the list will help you to weed out the problem and encourage growth beyond the failure.

1. Communication breakdown

2. Absence of trust

3. Unresolved conflict

4. Mass exodus of talent

5. Withdrawals

6. Becoming too comfortable

7. Lack of decision making

8. Tattling

9. Blame and lack of responsibility

10. Silos

11. Avoidance of vulnerability

12. Workload imbalance

13. Scapegoating and subgroups

14. Fixating on past and current problems

We've learned why teams fail and that it is acceptable to fail. The true catastrophes occur when you can't see progress or acceptance and the drama never fades. Only you can create a JoyPowered™ mindset that sets the tone to gain loyalty, trust, vulnerability, and communication, which will teach you and your team how to handle any success or failure.

Action Items

1. Write down up to three warning signs that you currently see on your work team. Assign a reason to each; for example, lack of trust, ego, lack of respect, loyalty, or communication.

2. List two ideas for how to address the failure for each warning sign. For example: *The reason for the lack of decision making is due to the lack of communication on the team. I will address the team members involved and set clear expectations on moving forward with all decisions, including dates and tasks. I will meet separately with each member involved and ask if they are vested in the team and how I can assist in their growth in making team decisions.*

3. Write a letter or email to one of your great leaders, whether it be a boss, a coach, a mentor, etc. Tell them what skills you admire and how they helped to shape your career. How can you continue to imitate them, create success, and yet lead teams that are not afraid to fail?

Can a Team Be Turned Around?

"If you are lucky enough to be someone's employer, then you have a moral obligation to make sure people do look forward to coming to work in the morning."

– John Mackey[45]

Yes! Yes! Yes indeed! Did you hear that? *"Yes!"* is the short but powerful answer to the question of whether a failing team can be turned around. And there are plenty of formerly struggling companies who weathered the transformation from broken to JoyPowered™ that are happy to share their stories. In this chapter, we will focus on some common discoveries among struggling companies – some Purple Ink clients and some world-renowned companies – that propelled their workforces into greater development, engagement, and productivity – into greater JoyPower!

First, let's establish that turning a team around can sometimes be a quick and painless process. Recently, Purple Ink outsourced one of our human resources experts to a client in transition. The company, while known for its rapid growth and diversity, was lacking an

HR Manager equipped to lead the charge. Human resources was deemed a necessary function, but not one that drives innovation. The previous manager had become an information hoarder, reducing her support circle to a small few. Employee morale was suffering, and people sought answers outside of HR. Needless to say, the dynamic lacked the energy of JoyPower. For ninety days, our HR expert worked onsite, providing our professional JoyPowered™ HR services for the client.

After only a couple of weeks, our Purple Ink HR consultant began to increase communication, demonstrating a willingness to serve, and intentionally connecting with departments like payroll, sales, and marketing. Gradually, more employees began visiting the HR department with questions and requests for assistance. Such healthy interaction had not been generated by HR in quite some time. In general, the culture of the organization was friendly and leadership modeled an open door policy, but that had not been evident in HR.

Purple Ink completed a few key projects that helped reframe the human resources function as a business partner and thought leader, reestablishing trust in the department. The JoyPower was returning, and senior leadership recognized it. When the new HR Manager came on board, the transition was much smoother than it might have been if engagement, trust, and most importantly, joy had not been present. It is undeniable: JoyPower can start anywhere in the organization, and it can start with you!

The Road from Misery to Joy

Gallup® has been studying workforce productivity and employee engagement for over fifty years. If you ask the folks at Gallup® about the secret to turning a team around, they'll likely mention four necessary areas for team improvement:[46]

1. Establishing role clarity

2. Investing in the development of the employee

3. Connecting the team to a higher mission and purpose

4. Valuing the advancement of employees as part of the team's central mission

The overarching recommendation at Gallup®, of course, is that a team in transformation adopt the CliftonStrengths® approach to positive team dynamics. To most effectively improve, a team must adopt the process of becoming strengths-based.[4] Gallup® believes that discovering and playing to the strengths of every employee will accomplish greater engagement, passion, and productivity at work.

Daniel Pink, author of numerous books on leadership and development, proposes three key components for turning a team around:[47]

1. Autonomy

2. Mastery

3. Purpose

Pink adds one essential caveat. Autonomy, mastery, and purpose can only be tackled after the topic of money, a basic motivator, has been satisfied and taken

joypowered

out of the equation. In other words, you won't really succeed in turning a team around until you've guaranteed a fair and competitive salary for all employees.

How does this translate into steps you can take to transform your team? Let's examine some discoveries and strategies for reversing negative trends among work teams.

Evaluating the Quality of Managers

VitalSmarts suggests that performance has less to do with processes, systems, and perks, and everything to do with people. What's more, Gallup® will tell you that when young professionals feel supported by their boss, their happiness on the job soars, as does company success.[48, 49] Millennials will make up 50% of the American workforce in less than a year – 2020![28] That's the demographic we should focus on when it comes to team transformation.

Two important comments on the designation *millennial* before we continue:

1. *Millennial* refers to anyone born between 1981 and 1996, ages 23 to 38 in 2019.[50]

2. When I mention *millennials*, I do so with utmost respect for the value this age demographic adds to the workplace. As a parent of four daughters born within the millennial time frame, I am inspired daily by their passion, drive, and astute self-awareness. Millennials inspire hope for the future of JoyPowered™ workspaces, teams and families.

Who leads your team(s)? We cannot emphasize enough the importance of a well-trained, people-oriented, culture-conscious team leader in creating a JoyPowered™ workspace. Gallup's report reveals that bosses carry the responsibility for 70% of employee engagement variances. Meanwhile, engaged bosses are 59% more likely to retain engaged employees.[49]

"The supportive behaviors of these managers to engage their employees included being accessible for discussion, motivating by strengths over weaknesses and helping to set goals. According to the Gallup® report, the primary determiner of employee retention and engagement are those in leadership positions. The boss is poised to affect employee happiness, satisfaction, productivity and performance directly." [49]

Or, you could consider abolishing the position of team manager altogether. That's precisely what Zappos[51] and Menlo[52] have done, and their joy factor has never been higher.

In 2013, Zappos' CEO, Tony Hsieh, began overhauling the structure of his online shoe sales company, moving it in the direction of what is called a Holacracy. A Holacracy can be defined as "a method of decentralized management and organizational governance, in which authority and decision-making are distributed throughout a holarchy of self-organizing teams rather than being vested in a management hierarchy." According to Hsieh, a company is better able to deliver happiness to both employees and customers when authority and decision-making are distributed

joypowered

throughout the organization. Teams at Zappos became self-organizing, rather than being vested in a management hierarchy. What we described as a JoyPowered™ team in this book, according to Hsieh, is a team full of leaders stepping up, taking their piece of the organization, and running with it with more autonomy and self-direction.

What continues to amaze is that the Zappos experiment worked! Zappos discovered that the more self-directed the team became, the more motivated, engaged, and productive it became. And, most importantly, the more successful they became at delivering their number one goal – customer satisfaction – delivering happiness within the company and beyond.

A similar success was experienced at a company called Menlo Innovations. In 1997, then vice-president Richard Sheridan bleakly contemplated how he was going to survive ten more years of grueling work, extended hours, and increasing pressures at a tech company that delivered custom software. Then came his epiphany – the value of joy! Sheridan decided to explore how joy could be a deliverable in the workplace.

One of the first things Sheridan did was to break down both the physical and hierarchical structures of the company. He invited all of his employees to abandon their offices, cubicles, desks, privacy, and positions of leadership, and join him in a huge warehouse-like room with collapsible tables, folding chairs, and shared computers (two people per computer). Gradually and voluntarily, employees trickled into the seeming melee of that décor-less empty space, where something magical began to spread: excitement, engagement,

autonomy, self-development, community, shared vision, fun, AND better customer service and increased productivity. Sheridan, the only "boss" in the organization, sits among his team of 50+ employees, hardly distinguishable in position or power from the rest of the group.

Today, people travel from far and wide to observe and learn the Menlo way – the way to a team where joy is a priority. Menlo Innovations' home page reads:

"Joy is designing and building something that actually sees the light of day and is enjoyably used and widely adopted by the people for whom it was intended. Beyond the joy of delivering high-quality software to our clients, the most gratifying part of our work are the stories of the impact that our software and process has on our clients, users, and our team. We call this The Menlo Effect."[53]

Employees today do not want bosses. Rather, they want coaches (see chapter two). The approach of a traditional-style boss is command and control – two strategies that are proving counter-productive to JoyPowered™ processes. Today's workers respond better to managers who can coach them, value them as people and employees, and help them understand and build their strengths.

If a team manager is unable to ride the wave of this first recommended step toward JoyPower, then the time has come for the individual to part ways with your organization. No one wants to have that difficult conversation, but the cost of *not* having it is just too

joypowered

great. You cannot turn the tide of evolving preferences in the workplace, and honestly, why would you want to? Millennials demand what we have all been craving – a deeper and richer experience of work – and we have been too slow to recognize the value of that expectation.

In her book, *No Ego*, author-speaker Cy Wakeman emphasizes that "buy-in" is a verb, and you can only work with the willing.[41] Particularly if you are an owner of a company, you must decide if employees are a good fit. If they are unable to evolve with the team and positively contribute to improving the quality of work and life for you and your team, then they cannot remain a part of the team.

Perhaps we can all learn a lesson from Zappos in this regard. When the decision was made to eliminate the management level at Zappos, those managers who could not weather the transition were presented with a respectful alternative. They were offered three months' salary to read Frederic Laloux's *Reinventing Organizations*. If they were not on board with the company's plan for transitioning according to the book's recommendations, they could quit. This concept was not new to Zappos. The online shoe company had long been offering compensation for new employees to quit if they could not espouse Zappos' now foundational self-management style.

Your company might not be in a position to propose so generous a bargain as Zappos for outgoing employees. However, a creative alternative that demonstrates appreciation and good faith could soften the blow in parting ways when employees are not a good culture fit.

Care, Trust, Love

"Leadership is not about being in charge. Leadership is about taking care of those in your charge."

- Simon Sinek

Team leaders often take a detached, stoic, all-business approach to their teams. Yet research shows that the leader who cares is the leader who effectively motivates and engages employees. Forbes magazine contributor John Hall claims that if you're completely avoiding a personal connection with your employees, you're making a big mistake. The possibility of joy will elude your team.

"Employees who feel valued and appreciated by their leaders are infinitely more likely to go above and beyond for the company and hold themselves accountable for their part of a project. Most importantly, they will be happier in their roles. If leaders disregard the importance of connecting with employees, they lose the benefit of a dedicated, long-term team."[54]

- John Hall

Hand-in-hand with care, a good manager develops trust among team members. The biggest challenge for leadership, according to Richard Sheridan of Menlo, is connecting with your teams. You have to build trust, which can only be done over time. Authenticity is one of the most important elements of leading a team from

joypowered

dysfunction to JoyPower. Leaders must understand themselves first and bring their real selves to work; not the selves they want to be, but the people they are. Building trust is about using the best part of yourself to lead the people who really want to follow, who want to be effectively guided and developed.

Trust is all about human-centered values practiced and expected in the workplace: leading with humility, speaking the truth, keeping your word, being consistent, demonstrating loyalty to your team. The trustworthy employee, whether a manager or a co-worker, is one you can place your confidence in, knowing without a doubt that he or she will not disappoint or betray you. Trust is the glue that holds a JoyPowered™ team together.

"And, over all these things put on love" (Col 3:14).[55] Yes, you read that right. Love. Love in the workplace. And taken right from the Bible. Love for your co-workers. Love, an essential ingredient of a JoyPowered™ team. Love, a virtue espoused by your entire team from the manager on down.

Richard Sheridan, the CEO of Menlo, was compelled to devote an entire chapter to the topic of love in his second book, *Chief Joy Officer*.[56] Inspiration for the chapter were the biblical verses, 1 Corinthians 13:4-7:

"Love is patient and kind; love is not jealous or boastful; it is not arrogant or rude. Love does not insist on its own way; it is not irritable or resentful; it does not rejoice at wrong but rejoices in the right. Love bears all things,

believes all things, hopes all things, endures all things."[57]

"Doesn't that say it all?" asks Sheridan. If we were all of these things for our team, wouldn't joy be the result? Not only does Sheridan believe this, but he has proven it through the Menlo Effect.

So, *care, trust, love*. How can a team striving to create a JoyPowered™ community sew these lofty yet practical virtues into the fabric of its behavior? According to VitalSmarts, the steps you take to re-pattern behaviors should follow two essential principles:[48]

Principle Number One: When faced with a number of possible options, take care to search for strategies that focus on specific behaviors.

Principle Number Two: Discover a few vital (high leverage) behaviors; change those, and problems – no matter the size – topple like cards.

Likewise, take care that the new behaviors you encourage in your fledgling JoyPowered™ team operate on the basis of two universal mental maps that we all share:

    1. Will it be worth it? (Am I motivated?)

    2. Can I do what's required of me? (Am I able?)

Once you convince your team members that they can buy into whatever behaviors you adopt, and that the effort will be worth it in moving from mediocre to JoyPowered™, then the transformation and the fun begin.

Of course, you should brainstorm with your own team to determine the particular vital behaviors of *care, trust,* and *love* that inspire greater joy among you. Including the team in this process is pivotal. Buy-in will increase as the team becomes more democratic in the process of decision-making.[58]

The following are some behaviors to get you started in turning your team from dysfunctional to JoyPowered™.

Care

- Eliminate all pedestals, both for owners and for managers. No one gets a special parking place. Everyone pours their own coffee, butters their own bagel, cleans their own dishes, carries their own files, etc. Unless, of course, a team member voluntarily offers to do any of the aforementioned.

- Back each other up with clients, projects, and tasks. Possible questions: "Which tasks on that project don't match your strengths, and how can I help?" "Can I help you with that contentious client you mentioned?" "Is there a piece of that project I can help you with so you can meet the deadline?"

- Ask caring questions of each other. Some ideas: "What are your hobbies?" "How is your spouse/partner?" "What are your children's names and where do they go to school?" "What sports do you like to watch?" "Whose concerts do you like to go to?" "What's your favorite snack?"

- Help one another outside of work. "Can I give you a ride to the airport?" "Do you need help with that deck you're building?" "I heard you're moving and I have a van - how can I help you?"

- Make time regularly to have breakfast or lunch with each team member. Set specific intervals for this and get the dates on your calendar way ahead of time.

Trust

- Tell the truth. When team members ask for feedback, no beating around the bush. Be honest, tactful, and kind at the same time. Deliver your message with what Purple Ink calls *feedforward* information. The *feedforward* approach raises the concept of feedback to a higher and more productive level. It turns the "Whose fault is this mistake?" attitude into a more creative and future-focused dialogue, centered on how we can take what we've learned and build a better solution together. This approach toward the truth acknowledges shortcomings and failures while also turning them into lessons for greater potential and growth.

- Have each other's backs.

- Keep your word. Honor due dates and deadlines.

- Make promises that are reasonable and deliverable.

- Never disappoint a team member by failing to live up to your commitments.

Love

- Show every team member that you value them. Affirm the strengths and gifts that each member brings to the team and point them out in action. When team members know they are valued, they will strive for excellence and make every effort not to disappoint each other.

- As often as possible, place the good of each other above your own individual good. This means being willing to make sacrifices of your own time and energy to accomplish what's good for others and for the team.

- Celebrate every accomplishment and win. Shout-out to co-workers who have done something special. Send personal notes of appreciation and encouragement (a well-worded email is all it takes). Take every opportunity to remark about what's good and positive about people, projects, awards, successes, etc.

- Permit and own mistakes. "Fess up," as they say, when you've failed. Tackle mistakes as soon as they surface. Forgive quickly. Move forward together as a team. No one is perfect, so expect slip-ups, misjudgments, errors. Let your team be real. Let your team be human. Love them for all of it.

Ensure Role Clarity

Setting performance expectations and specific job tasks is fundamental to a JoyPowered™ culture. Team

members perform with greater excellence when they know what's expected of them. And when they do know what's expected of them, teams are more invested and engaged in the effort of the whole team.

I recently interviewed a young woman, Annie, about her sales experience with a start-up tech company. Annie was passionate about her company's mission; so passionate that she stuck it out through months of upheaval as the company increased from 100 to 500 employees. "They were completely unprepared for the growing sales team and increase in sales expectations," explained Annie, a sales rep at that point. "Their philosophy was to hire *non-sales-y* people. *Smart, fun, and nice* were strengths they were going for in their sales reps. That worked while they were small, but *smart, fun, and nice* did not translate into an efficient and productive sales team in the midst of a 500% increase in employee base.

"From one day to the next, I did not know what my job assignment was going to be. Often it switched several times a day. And there was no training to keep up with the changes. It was just like, 'Here's what we need you to do now. We hired you because you're smart. You can figure it out.' Only I couldn't figure it out, because I had no context for what was assigned to me. No one knew how to visualize, analyze, or strategize. Leadership also kept changing roles in the hopes that someone would surface with the skills we needed to grow sales as we grew our employee base."

You'll be happy to learn that Annie's workplace weathered the storm and is in a much better place today, mostly due to the positive culture and trusted leadership. But it certainly speaks to the importance of

role clarity. Annie was bounced around like a rubber ball and came critically close to quitting.

In your efforts to turn your team around, take care to evaluate every position on the team, incorporating its goals and objectives as well as the duties and responsibilities of the position.

- Describe the skills and strengths required for the position.

- Hire individuals who have the potential, training, and experience in applying those skills and strengths to the job.

- Align the goals and objectives of the position to the team's goals and objectives as a whole.

- Specify the daily, weekly, monthly expectations involved and how they interface with responsibilities of other employees up and down the ladder.

A corollary to ensuring role clarity is providing ongoing and specific feedforward information to every team member. Recall that feedforward information refers to two-way communication that enhances the development of skills and performance in employees for future success. Today's employees desire continuous evaluation on performance for maximum development of potential. We recommend a minimum of four feedforward meetings per year between a manager and an employee.

In Gallup's 2016 study on millennials, they discovered that only 21% of young professional employees meet weekly with their boss and 17% receive meaningful

feedback.[59] The most positive engagement booster occurred when managers focused on employee strengths. In the end, one out of every two employees will leave a job to get away from their boss when they're unsupported. Not only will ongoing performance information raise the joy factor on your team, but it will save you money in lost revenue from poor retention.

Increase Autonomy of Team Members

Research shows that satisfaction and happiness increase when employees are given greater autonomy. Autonomy refers to the amount of freedom that employees are permitted while they are working. The more autonomy you can build into your work culture, the greater the JoyPower you will notice developing.

As much as possible, a team should be encouraged to self-direct regarding their own goals, objectives, development, and work style. When you can give your team carte blanche on how and when they accomplish their tasks, the results are impressive. Granted, the nature of some businesses does not lend itself to employees deciding on, for example, their own hours. But as I sit here working at 7:00 in the evening, I'm certainly grateful that my job permits me to work when I am most creative. For me, that's generally in the evening. I don't know why, but I've been that way since high school. You're just not going to get the passion and quality from me at 7:00 a.m. that you will get at 7:00 p.m. So, that's when I do my best work.

What about your team? Do you encourage them to make their own decisions rather than micromanage them? Begin by asking them to create monthly, quarterly, and yearly goals. Then, encourage them to

keep on task by checking in with them every couple of months. Frequent goals-focused meetings with your team members guarantee an increase in JoyPower, precisely because it accomplishes two purposes: frequent one-on-one time with each team member; and team members, motivated by your attention, who are more likely to stay on goal through your frequent touchpoints.

In general, greater team autonomy fosters an increase in work quality and job satisfaction. Employees take more responsibility for outcomes and team culture. The very idea of delegating authority to team members gives them a sense of value and dignity that pushes them to perform better.

Naturally, there will always be employees whose performance actually diminishes as autonomy increases. Some team members might require closer oversight, imposed deadlines, and daily direction on tasks. The success or failure of such employees will depend on whether or not you and the other team members can tolerate both work styles on the same team. Only you can decide if such individuals are a good fit for the JoyPowered™ team you are trying to create.

Connect Jobs to the Company's Mission

A company's purpose or mission is an affirmation of its reason for being in business. According to Gallup®:

"Having a strong mission and purpose also instills a sense of pride in employees. As part of a positive and idealistic generation, millennials want to understand how their jobs fit into the grander scheme of things — and they want to feel good about that connection.

A company's purpose matters to millennial employees — and all employees — but in the workplace, Gallup® data reveals that slightly more than one in three millennial workers strongly agree that the mission or purpose of their organization makes them feel their job is important."[59]

When Annie was describing her experience at that tech company, her voice took on a distinct joy and enthusiasm every time she mentioned the company's mission – to simplify the selection process of insurance packages specific to the needs of the insured. One thing her company did well was to evangelize their mission to every employee and gain buy-in that superseded any complaints about their growing pains. They managed to keep some pretty talented personnel through their tumultuous growth, including a manager who was able to stabilize and strategize their sales functions.

Invest in the Development of Team Members

Your employees are your greatest asset. Your commitment to them is demonstrated through the investment you are willing to make in their development. Eighty-seven percent of young professionals rate "professional or career growth and development opportunities" as important to them in a job.[59]

Author Brigette Tasha Hyacinth asks her readers to consider: Instead of just focusing on the bottom line, why not invest in the people responsible for the bottom line? At the University of Pennsylvania, researchers discovered that businesses that spent 10% of their revenue on capital improvements saw a 3.9% productivity increase. But when that same 10% was invested in employees, productivity went up 8.5%.[60]

Employees are the heartbeat of the company, declares Hyacinth. And if the heart stops beating...what will happen?

How does a company go about investing in employee development? We recommend that, in the spirit of increasing the autonomy of your employees, you ask them! Begin with these prompts:

- What are your strengths and how can we help you improve on them?

- What training opportunities would help you develop greater passion for your current position?

- What are your goals for yourself here?

- What training opportunities would help you move toward your career goals here?

- What kind of training would make you more valuable to this company and why?

There are many ways you can go about this conversation. The important issues are the financial resources you are willing to allocate to employee development. The ball is in your court regarding the JoyPowered™ development of your team! Just do it!

We asked the question at the beginning of this chapter, "Can a team be turned around?" The answer is a resounding yes! A struggling team can be turned around, but it takes your JoyPowered™ leadership. When you focus on bringing out the best in each staff member and enabling them to feel connection with the company, the mission, and the team, you are well on your way to a JoyPowered™ team.

Action Items

1. Provide training opportunities that would help your team members develop greater passion for their contribution to the team.

2. Interview your team members to discover, document, and track their goals. Make their goals your goals.

3. Ensure your company mission is well-articulated, well-communicated, and fully embraced. Refer to it frequently, reciting it word for word.

Teams in Transition

"Diamonds are nothing more than chunks of coal that stuck to their jobs."

– Malcolm Forbes

SUSAN

The Bureau of Labor Statistics reported in September 2018 that the median number of years that workers stay with an employer is 4.2.[61] Your team may have a higher average length of tenure than that, but you will no doubt face people coming and going. Teams need to prepare themselves to survive during the almost inevitable team member transition. With dedicated focus, teams can be ready to handle composition changes and – if done really well – can be stronger because of it.

Navigating Emotions through Team Arrivals and Departures

Every sibling is born into a different family. The oldest sibling usually arrives in a house with brand new parents who need some quick on-the-job training and

who are focused on the miracle of them. The second sibling gets the benefit of a more experienced set of parents, but they have a brother or sister competing for their attention. If you are like me, the youngest of six, the family you join is remarkably different than the one your oldest sibling met – one which now has all the dynamics associated with a group of eight very different individuals. Likewise, no associate joins the same team. Every new staff member you bring in and every person who leaves your team changes the essence of the group and can have a strong emotional impact on all the team members.

In 1969, Elisabeth Kubler-Ross introduced the five stages of grief when a loved one dies – shock/denial, anger, bargaining, depression, and acceptance. She later partnered with David Kessler to expand the usage of these stages to any kind of personal loss in their 2005 book, *On Grief and Grieving: Finding the Meaning of Grieving through the 5 Stages of Loss.*[62]

While perhaps not as traumatic as a personal loss, the transition of a team member can have a similarly profound effect. When someone joins a team, usually colleagues appreciate the help, and although they need to get to know the individual, they are glad the person has arrived. When someone leaves, it can trigger a wide range of emotions: *relief* if the person wasn't pulling his or her weight, *sadness* that a friend is leaving, *concern* that maybe you should be looking for a new job too, *anger* that you now need to help train someone new and carry a heavier workload until she or he is found, or *shock* that the person was not as content to stay as you are.

Managers need to recognize that new team members coming, and especially team members going, affect every team member in their own unique way. Give people time to express what they are feeling, acknowledge it, and involve them in fortifying the new team.

I can vividly recall a team change where I progressed through the multiple stages of loss. I received a call from a boss I really liked letting me know that he was leaving the company. He was one of the very best HR leaders and people I knew. He wasn't on the best of terms with the senior business leader we supported, as they often had different opinions on the approach to people issues.

I remember my shock that our company would let someone possessing such knowledge and capability walk away without trying to find a role where his talents could be utilized. I couldn't imagine how our team was going to survive his departure, especially when I learned his replacement was a woman who had no HR experience, but did enjoy a good rapport with the senior business leader we supported. I soon became angry, thinking that this company didn't value its HR professionals and therefore, through extension, me. Didn't they realize technical knowledge and experience handling people concerns were critical skills, or did they think just anyone could do it?

I then moved to the bargaining phase. Maybe our new leader wouldn't change how we were doing things. She'd recognize we knew what we were doing and wouldn't mess with success. Then changes started happening in rapid succession. Our focus changed, we were assigned new priorities, and depression settled in; I began thinking that maybe this wasn't the job for me.

Fortunately, acceptance began to emerge. Before long, I started to see how my new boss, having the respect of the top business leader, enabled us to implement initiatives more quickly. HR was now becoming an integral player in actively assisting a line of business to achieve its objectives. I found myself, who I thought was a strong HR professional, developing into a better business person. I not only got to the acceptance stage in the Kubler-Ross curve, I felt like our team was stronger because of the change.

Lastly, leaders need to be cognizant that not everyone on the existing team may be thrilled to welcome a new colleague. Co-workers may be asking, "What does this mean for me? What if this person is better than I am? How does this change my place in the company? What if they change the way we do things?" Being present, listening, and supporting when these feelings surface can help the staff member who is feeling vulnerable get to the acceptance stage quicker.

Assimilating New Team Members

The best way to strengthen a team with a newly arrived associate is to ensure that the new colleague is truly welcomed, has the opportunity to bond, is brought up to speed on job responsibilities, and is fully integrated into company culture.

We asked HR professionals how they effectively absorb new employees. The responses varied widely:

"We don't do a lot" – Anonymous

"Make sure the basics are covered: bathrooms, lunches, start/end time, how to get help. Then we focus on the work." – Jen S.

> *"[We have new hires work] out of conference rooms instead of cubicles when they first start. [We ask] them questions, not just to check and see how their work is going, but also to get to know more about them."* – Anonymous

> *"[We give them] lots of one-on-one time, asking questions about their concerns, helping connect with others."* - Nancy

Much has been written about the importance of onboarding a new staff member effectively. The SHRM Foundation's 2010 *Onboarding New Employees: Maximizing Success* reported that "New employees who are part of a well-structured onboarding orientation program are 69% more likely to remain at a company for up to three years."[63]

A game changer for companies is to recognize that the onboarding process begins from the moment the new hire utters the words, "I accept," to the job offer, and some would even say it begins when the candidate applies to your opening. The employee experience can be forever influenced by actions taken or not taken at the get go.

The Hiring Manager cannot go radio silent until the new hire shows up on day one. Once the HR representative has the accepted offer, the hiring manager ideally reaches out to the new hire to welcome him or her to the team and celebrate the decision. The more touches the new hire receives before day one on the job, the better. Touches can be as simple as a quick call, email, or text to let them know you are thinking of them and counting the days until their arrival. *The Muse* Founder Kathryn Minshew says, "Sending them benefits

information and your employee handbook ahead of their first day gives them a chance to get acquainted with the culture before they step in the door."

Consider identifying a co-worker to be the new hire's buddy and have him or her ready to greet the new associate at the door on the first day. Make sure the person's first day is truly welcoming and that at least their first few weeks are mapped out so they get a chance to spend quality time with new colleagues, management, clients, and support areas. In this way, they'll have the opportunity to make the personal connections that will serve them well.

I met JoDee Curtis, the owner of Purple Ink, LLC and one of the co-authors of this book, at the beginning of 2014 just as I was beginning my "encore career" of HR consulting. JoDee had been in business as an HR Consultant for four years before I met her, after she had a successful career in public accounting and corporate HR. At the time, JoDee had just hired her first full-time staff member a few months before. I felt an immediate connection to her – maybe because we share two of our top five strengths, Positivity and Maximizer, and we both wanted to do joyful HR work.

Since that fateful day when we met for coffee at a Starbucks, I have watched JoDee's firm grow to her current team of thirteen amazing people: seven full-time and four part-time employees, along with two regular contractors. I am one of her two regular contractors and call myself a Purple Ink Collaborator. One of the first things JoDee did after onboarding several staff members was to build a New Hire Assimilation program. She asked the newest members of the team what would have been helpful to know when joining Purple Ink. The

team created an eighty-page New Employee Guide as well as a four-week onboarding schedule to help new staff members navigate that first month socially and build relationships. JoDee now assigns a mentor to each new hire. The following is the week by week Onboarding Plan at Purple Ink:

WEEK ONE

1. Go to lunch with your mentor.
2. Explore the office.
3. Familiarize yourself with Dropbox.
4. Write your bio for website.
5. Meet with CliftonStrengths® coach on assessment results.
6. Follow Purple Ink on social media.
7. Get picture taken for website.

WEEK TWO

1. Learn names of five co-workers.
2. Write a blog.
3. Review Purple Ink Employee Manual.
4. Listen to The JoyPowered™ Workspace Podcast
5. Review View My Paycheck instructions.
6. Take someone else to lunch.

WEEK THREE

1. Schedule a meeting with JoDee and tell her how things are going.

2. Learn the Purple Ink values and share what you know with a co-worker.

3. Schedule a meeting with an HR Consultant to ask questions and learn more about what they do at Purple Ink.

4. Learn the rest of the names of co-workers.

5. Review Purple Ink's website and ask a co-worker a question about something you read.

WEEK FOUR

1. Schedule your 45-day meeting with JoDee so you can tell her how things are going.

2. Recite the Purple Ink values by heart.

3. Ask someone to review their own development plan with you.

4. Go to lunch with someone else.

5. Schedule meetings with two co-workers to learn about what they do at Purple Ink.

New hires at Purple Ink feel connected to the mission, vision, and values within their first month, and are connected to the other staff members through this thoughtful and intentional onboarding process.

Team Members Exiting Involuntarily

There are times when the healthiest thing to do for a team is to ask one of the staff members to leave.

joypowered

Perhaps the individual isn't performing up to expectations, or following company policy, or they aren't demonstrating the values of the organization. Paul Spiegelman, Chief Culture Officer at Stericycle, wrote an article for *Inc.* called *Why You Need to Fire Bad Employees Right Now*, identifying a few critical ways a poor performing staff member can undermine the work environment:[64]

- He or she can threaten the morale of your other employees.

- Bad employees do second-rate work and bring others down with them, reducing overall productivity.

- People who aren't engaged don't provide the best service, and your customers will take notice.

- If you aren't willing to make the tough decisions, your good employees will lose trust and respect for you.

A word of caution: These examples of job-terminating dysfunction are profound and can generate a certain amount of vindictiveness, possibly generating the desire by management to make an example of the terminated employee. This approach must be resisted at all costs. Indeed, the HR professional should not share the specifics as to why a team member departs.

There have been many times when I have helped business leaders terminate an employee because the individual has violated a major company policy, a code of ethics, or committed some other act where immediate termination was the only appropriate course of action. In a number of those cases, I would have managers

say, "Susan, we need to make this a public execution so everyone knows what the ex-staff-member did, and they're warned what will happen if they ever do anything similar."

As disappointed as you and the manager may be in what the person did, you don't want to share someone's private termination details publicly. The best advice is to take a breath and revisit how you are communicating what terminable actions are. Is there an opportunity to better explain what is allowed, what is not, and what the consequences are? Is there a need to develop additional training or amplify these kinds of issues in existing training?

When someone is released from their job, the fact is that teammates will know the individual is gone and not coming back. It makes sense to build a communication plan that will fortify remaining staff and allay fears that they may be next.

Once the departing employee has been removed from the work environment, it is time to pull together the remaining team members, let them know the person (let's call her Mary) is gone, talk about the plan to either replace her or reallocate her work load, answer questions and – short of discussing Mary's shortcomings – explain how the future will be brighter now. If individuals make comments wondering why it took so long for Mary to leave, refocus the conversation on moving the team forward.

When a colleague's employment ends and they're viewed as culpable through lack of effort or bad behavior, co-workers usually don't feel badly about it. It's a justified departure and the exiting employee is simply "getting what's coming to them." However,

joYpowered

situations aren't always clear cut. Sometimes, team members who felt personally connected to the departing staff member may experience "survivor's guilt." Colleagues may feel badly that they survived in the workplace and someone else didn't. Restructuring, reduction in force, off-shoring, or outsourcing of a function are all examples of exit-causing events that are often viewed as happening through no fault of the individual involved – you can feel guilty that your job remains while the other person's does not. We asked HR and business leaders, "What do you do to help remaining team members through survivor's guilt if you see it surface?" and they told us:

> *"We don't do much outside of informing the team and mak[ing] ourselves available for questions should anyone in the team have any."* – Anonymous

> *"Usually when a team member is terminated, there isn't survivor's guilt. Team members know when a co-worker is not productive, and usually there is relief that the team can move ahead more efficiently/effectively."* – Jen S.

> *"Transparency as much as possible without violating confidentiality. Giving team members time to mourn and letting them have some say in the reorganization of work that they may have to assume."* – Nancy G.

> *"Explain the process behind the decision to terminate [and] the opportunities for them and new hires to fill the void."* – Anonymous

In the large financial institution I worked at most of my career, I saw many wonderful people who were better

at what they did than I was get laid off when work became redundant. This was due to mergers and acquisitions, business units moving to centralized strategic sites, operations being off-shored, people expenses needing to be reduced when revenues were down, etc. You can't help but feel badly when you survive while someone you admire and respect loses his or her role through no fault of their own.

There were countless events – mergers, acquisitions, restructuring, major shifts in strategy -- when I was certain that my job was coming to an end. I would come home and share my concerns with my husband so often that he eventually recognized these end-of-the-world pronouncements as something of a routine. However, after 35 years, a major change occurred, and sure enough, I was laid off. It took 35 years, but I was eventually right!

The most effective way to reduce survivor's guilt is to make sure the remaining team members know that their departing staff members are being well cared for during this time of employment transition. Put thought and energy into creating an outplacement program that everyone in the company knows about. Consider including:

- **Severance Pay** to ensure the individual can meet immediate bills and has reasonable time to locate a new job.

- **Benefit Continuation** through the severance pay period before going on COBRA where full costs and administrative fees can make it cost prohibitive for many.

joXxowered

- **Career Coaching** services to build an effective resume, learn to navigate job boards, update a LinkedIn profile, market oneself, be refreshed on interviewing skills, and land that next job.

- **Financial Planning** advice from an independent third party who can help the individual determine how best to weather this financial setback and make good decisions with their money.

- **Employee Assistance Program** to help counsel the departing staff member and/or their family members to deal with the emotions around losing the security of the job and embarking on this major life change.

As part of my HR consulting practice, I spent three years working with Mullin International as a contract career coach and the last year and a half as a part-time career consultant with Lee Hecht Harrison (LHH) after they bought Mullin International. My role is to be a coach for someone who has just learned that his or her employer, a client of LHH, is eliminating their job. Depending on the client, and sometimes the level of the individual, I have anywhere from a month to a year to help that individual land a job. This work has been some of the most joyful work I have had the pleasure of doing.

The first time I speak to an individual I have been assigned, I assess where I think they are on the Kubler-Ross curve and then I try to support them getting to acceptance. I have witnessed how someone who is full of self-doubt and afraid they will never find an employer who values them again can transform into a confident job seeker who can articulate their worth. Co-workers who see former colleagues receiving coaching as part

of a robust outplacement program recognize their company will treat them respectfully if they end up being laid off in the future.

Team Members Exiting by Choice

Gallup's 2017 State of the American Workplace says 51% of American workers are actively looking for a different job or watching for openings right now.[65] More than half of your team members may be on the hunt for their next role, and certainly some will leave you. How can you strengthen a team when someone leaves it if you were not expecting or hoping they would leave?

First, celebrate the fact that you have helped develop people who are now going out into the wider world with more experience and more skills than they had when you hired them. They have a chance now to continue their growth and be a brand ambassador for you as an employer. Smart businesses invite departing team members to join their LinkedIn Alumni groups so they have an avenue to continue communicating with their former employees. EY has done a good job on this front. EY is a global enterprise of 200,000 employees and has a global alumni footprint of over 800,000 people who have moved from EY to other businesses. These 800,000 former employees are now a formidable group of potential business referrals, applicant referrals, and/or rehire possibilities.

Rehires, sometimes called boomerang employees because they have left and then returned, can be a morale booster for teams. Someone who has gone out and found the grass may not have been greener helps the part of your workforce who is considering leaving realize, "Maybe this is a great place to work." The

returning staff member usually brings back fresh intelligence of what is happening outside of your shop that helps infuse new thinking, which can also ignite creativity on the team. Treating people well as they leave and making sure they know the door remains open if they want to return helps the entire team realize they are truly valued.

Be sure to take the time to conduct exit interviews with all staff members before they leave (and of course, stay interviews while they are still with you!). Exit interviews are an excellent opportunity to get their unbiased opinions on the best parts of your team, what needs improvement, and recommendations on how to attract and retain talent. By virtue of having spent time in your trenches, they know the good, the bad, and the ugly – ask them to enlighten you!

One of my favorite staff members ever was Tom. When Tom was on my team, he ran our company's multiple campus recruiting programs, handled difficult to fill professional roles, managed employee relations for a segment of the organization, and facilitated the company-wide employee activities programs — a particularly challenging responsibility which no one else wanted, as it often meant spending late nights at the basketball courts, mediating competitive flare-ups, etc. Tom was always upbeat, high-energy, and asking to do more. He was JoyPowered™ even before I knew what it meant!

After working together about six years, Tom was selected to go into a Finance Leadership program at our then out-of-state company headquarters. I was so happy for him, but sad for our team as I knew his leaving

was going to be a huge loss. I will never forget Tom telling me that in the several weeks remaining before his new role started, he planned to recruit for his replacement and hire him or her as quickly as possible because he wanted to personally train the person. And he did! Tom demonstrated for me what true commitment to a team looks like, especially in a time of transition. He has gone on to hold many challenging roles. I feel lucky that Tom and I have remained friends to this day.

Being Intentional in Your Succession Planning

While it's a rare team that can stay leaderless for long, there are successful organization models that migrate managerial supervision within the teams, as was discussed in chapter six.

Regardless of the approach, most companies recognize the benefit to having skilled, strong managers leading teams and feel the effect quickly when a manager position is vacant. We asked HR and business leaders if they do formal succession planning, and if so, to what degree. Their responses are captured in the following graphs.

JoyPowered Survey: How Would You Describe Your Current Succession Plan?

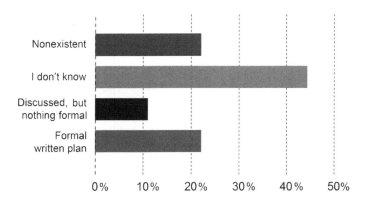

JoyPowered Survey: Which Roles Are Included in Your Written Succession Plan?

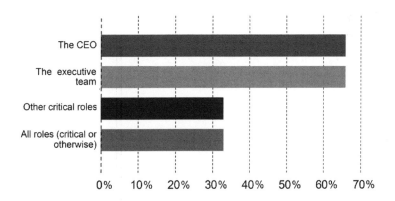

Succession planning can be as simple as ensuring that if your business head exited tomorrow, you have a vetted successor ready to replace him or her. In family-owned businesses where someone in the next

generation has been groomed their whole life for the role – and no one else in the family objects – you are finished and can live happily ever after! Unfortunately, the vast majority of companies don't live this fairy tale.

It is important to look at the entire leadership team and determine which roles, if vacant for any significant time, invite risk in your operation. Certainly, the C-Suite fits this description. An extended vacancy in the corporate suite poses risks and leaves a gaping hole in a company's core management team; the importance of a succession plan for top level management is obvious. With that said, it's equally important to not overlook other key roles residing deeper in the organization that if unfilled could have severe revenue, customer, regulatory compliance, or employee engagement impact. It may be the prodigious sales leaders, high impact account managers, high level internal auditors, and the effective people leaders for which a replacement strategy is crucial.

Once the critical roles are identified, a succession plan must be tailored for each unique situation. The following is a straightforward approach to designing a succession plan is presented.

Succession Plan Design Approach

Step 1

Action: Identify critical leadership competencies necessary to be a "fit" for your organization.

Tips: Pull ideas from the company's mission, vision, and values and have the executive team agree on the ten to twelve most critical.

joypowered

Examples: Able to drive change. Holds self and others accountable.

Step 2

Action: Analyze each role to identify the specific job competencies necessary to perform effectively.

Tips: Review the job description; talk to the incumbent and incumbent's manager. Confirm the six to eight technical knowledge and behavioral skills and abilities needed.

Examples: Engineering degree. Program management experience managing a multi-layer, cross functional team.

Step 3

Action: Determine internal feeder groups that may have incumbents that may be potential candidates for each role.

Tips: Look at colleagues and direct reports of the role, and any other high-potential staff member reporting to one of that role's colleagues who you know has transferable skills.

Examples: For the Chief HR Officer role, look at the entire executive team as to who might benefit from rotating into the role, the CHRO's direct reports, and other C-Suite high performing direct reports with transferable skills.

Step 4

Action: Have the direct manager assess each potential candidate on the leadership and technical competencies you identified in step two.

Tips: Add insights as to how soon the potential candidate may be ready to assume a higher role, whether the individual is a retention risk, and if they desire a higher-level role someday.

Step 5

Action: Assemble the executive team to discuss the potential candidates for each role and determine who is the most viable.

Tips: Have a facilitator ensure that the executive team is challenging each other's thinking, that "easy" or "hard" evaluators use this opportunity to calibrate, and that the team agrees.

Step 6

Action: If there is no viable internal candidate, turn the discussion to how to import talent.

OR, if the most viable internal candidate isn't "ready now" for a particular position, the executive team should map out an individual development plan that will ready the potential successor.

Tips: Depending on the probability of the role coming open soon, the executive team may wish

joypowered

to generate a list of external talent they know, consider using the next opening in that area to recruit an individual who could be a successor, or plan the timing of launching an external search.

OR, the most viable internal candidate is not told they are "the successor;" instead, they are being developed as a *potential* successor.

Step 7

Action: Annually review your succession planning process.

Tips: Ask yourself the following questions.

Are the critical roles still the right ones to include?

Has the succession plan been successfully used this past year? If not, why not?

Has progress been made on developing the viable internal candidates?

Are there new potential successor candidates that should be assessed?

Is it time to launch an external search for any role?

Purple Ink is currently consulting with a 300+ person company that is, and intends to always be, a JoyPowered™ team. They want to ensure continuity in their leadership. We helped this organization begin their succession planning efforts several years ago when they identified the top dozen or so critical senior roles in their operation. Once the succession plans for these

critical positions were established, we progressed to the next layer of high impact roles. And now, with succession plans being executed and revisited at the top layer of the firm on a regular basis, the executive team recognizes the fruit of their efforts: they have successors developed and ready deep in their organization who will fuel JoyPowered™ teams throughout their company. Their additional focus is now on roles that are difficult to fill, have a history of unusually high turnover, or single incumbent roles where the person is retirement eligible. This client has committed energy, thought leadership, and time to ensure smooth team transitions.

Teams are going to go through transitions with people coming and going. You can hope the resilience of the team will carry it through the good times and the bad, or you can choose to focus on embracing new team members, exiting people who need to go in a supportive way, and having strong succession plans at the ready.

Action Items:

1. Ask all your team members to reach out to new hires and personally focus on accelerating the new person's assimilation to your team.

2. When you let a person go for no fault of their own, provide the outplacement support that shows your remaining team members the level of commitment you have to all of them.

3. Be ready with qualified successors for the key roles in your company. Design your own succession planning approach now!

Epilogue

Now that you've spent time reading about JoyPowered™ teams and taking notes on the insights and actions that inspired you, it's time to send you forth!

DENISE

Go out and be the JoyPowered™ change you want to see in your workplace! Remember, JoyPower does NOT have to begin at the top. JoyPower starts with any and every individual who has the audacity to dream of a better team and the courage to take JoyPowered™ action. JoyPower begins with one person's choice to start small, to trust in the ripple effect of JoyPowered™ action, and to celebrate the outcome of JoyPowered™ efforts. JoyPower begins with YOU!

As for an epilogue to this book, you've already written that yourself! Turn to your chapter notes and your action plan and get started. There's no time like the present to infuse JoyPowered™ energy into your workplace.

Thank you for joining the JoyPowered™ movement!

Appendix A:
My Personal Notes on
The JoyPowered™ Team

I have gained the following insights from reading *The JoyPowered™ Team*:

Chapter 1: Why Team Matters

Insight 1 _____

_____

Insight 2 _____

_____

Chapter 2: Team Roles

Insight 1 _____

_____

Insight 2 _____

_____

Chapter 3: Embracing Team Diversity

Insight 1 _____

_____

Insight 2 _____

joy**powered**

_____

Chapter 4: Why Teams Succeed

    Insight 1 _____

    _____

    Insight 2 _____

    _____

Chapter 5: Why Teams Fail

    Insight 1 _____

    _____

    Insight 2 _____

    _____

Chapter 6: Can a Team Be Turned Around?

    Insight 1 _____

    _____

    Insight 2 _____

    _____

Chapter 7: Teams in Transition

    Insight 1 _____

    _____

    Insight 2 _____

    _____

Appendix B:
My JoyPowered™ Team
Action Plan

I will initiate the following actions to inspire a JoyPowered™ team in my workplace:

Immediately:

1. _____

2. _____

3. _____

4. _____

In One Month:

1. _____

2. _____

3. _____

4. _____

In Three Months:

1. _____

2. _____

3. _____

joypowered

4. _____

In Six Months:

1. _____

2. _____

3. _____

4. _____

In One Year:

1. _____

2. _____

3. _____

4. _____

Appendix C: About the Team

The JoyPowered™ Team was written by Erin Brothers, JoDee Curtis, Peggy Hogan, Denise McGonigal, Laura North, Susan Tinder White, and Liz Zirkelbach and edited by Emily Miller. They are teammates at Purple Ink LLC, a human resources consulting firm offering a wide variety of HR solutions, including consulting, recruiting, outsourcing, training, and career coaching. The group collaborated on this book to share the strategies and mindsets that have helped their team and others become JoyPowered™.

Learn more about Purple Ink at www.purpleinkllc.com.

joypowered

JoDee Curtis, SHRM-SCP, CPA

Maximizer, Arranger, Positivity, Strategic, Futuristic

About JoDee

JoDee Curtis is the Owner of Purple Ink and the ink pad, author of *JoyPowered™: Intentionally Creating an Inspired Workspace*, co-author of *The JoyPowered™ Family,* and co-host of The JoyPowered™ Workspace Podcast. JoDee has a passion for helping organizations and individuals discover their talents and do more of what they do best! JoDee is a wife and the mother of three humans and two labradoodles, and she loves to read and travel.

JoDee's Strength Contribution to the Book

My **Arranger** was bursting throughout the writing of this book! Gallup's definition of **Arranger** is *"one who organizes and likes to determine how all of the pieces and resources can be arranged for maximum productivity."* I volunteered to set the tone for the rest of the book by writing the first chapter. I loved gathering us together, leading the process, setting an agenda, asking for ideas, and keeping us on task. My **Maximizer** kept sneaking in to *"transform something strong into something superb"* and keep us productive.

Peggy Hogan, SHRM-SCP

Ideation, Woo, Includer, Communication, Adaptability

About Peggy

Peggy Hogan is the Manager of Career Transition Services at Purple Ink. She enjoys connecting the right person to the right place, whether she's career coaching, recruiting, or working on-site with a client. She is motivated to help create positive workspaces by offering creative solutions to problems. She is the wife of one, mother of three, dog mom of two, and Nana of one! Peggy loves to play tennis with friends and travel "up north" to Michigan.

Peggy's Strength Contribution to the Book

My **Communication** strength was on fire while working on the book! Gallup® says that people with **Communication** *"feel they must express themselves, and this expression can take many forms – verbally, artistically, musically, through writing or composition, how one dresses, teaches or even how one tells stories."* My **Communication** and **Ideation** strengths were fueled by collaborating with the team on the overall organization of the book, down to the details of choosing the best word for the message.

---

joypowered

Erin Brothers, SHRM-CP, PHR

Achiever, Communication, Strategic, Positivity, Activator

About Erin

Erin Brothers is the Director of Consulting Services at Purple Ink. Erin helps clients with HR needs through consulting, recruiting, outsourcing, and training. Erin loves helping clients understand how diversity and inclusion play a critical role in their organization.

Erin's Strength Contribution to the Book

I used my **Activator** strength to get me rolling on writing my chapter of *The JoyPowered™ Team*. The collaboration of the team during the writing process was unmatched. My passion for the topic of embracing diversity and my get-it-done attitude helped keep things moving. The opportunity to share my diversity journey is a life goal met!

Liz Zirkelbach

Responsibility, Relator, Arranger, Restorative, Significance

About Liz

Liz Zirkelbach is an HR Coordinator for Purple Ink LLC. Liz has a special interest in finding the perfect fit for a role and helping both the person and the company find their joy. Liz loves to craft candles, read, and do cardio.

Liz's Strength Contribution to the Book

My **Significance** theme made me want to get involved with writing this book. I felt it was important to tell our team's story in order to help other workplaces thrive. When it came time to write the book, my **Relator** theme really kicked in, because I love to tell stories about my experiences in the hope that others will resonate with my words.

---

joypowered

Laura North, SHRM-CP, PHR

Responsibility, Arranger, Relator, Belief, Learner

About Laura

Laura North is a Human Resources Consultant at Purple Ink. She uses her experience as a Benefits Specialist to resolve complex client issues. In addition to benefits, Laura works with clients to improve efficiencies in recruiting, onboarding, new hire training, payroll, and employee relations. Laura enjoys spending time in the great outdoors with her husband and two young sons.

Laura's Strength Contribution to the Book

I used my **Learner** strength throughout the duration of the book writing process. I wanted to absorb knowledge about why teams fail, and I could not stop reading books that created avenues that I wanted to pursue. The learning process of book writing and collaboration with the team was motivating each step of the way. Being vulnerable to feedback, honest, and trusting with the process confirmed why we began the work in the first place; to prove we truly have a JoyPowered™ team!

Denise McGonigal, MA

Achiever, Arranger, Learner, Connectedness, Responsibility

About Denise

Denise McGonigal is a trainer for Purple Ink and co-author of *The JoyPowered ™ Family*. She loves bringing leadership skills to life for businesses through dynamic workshops, and also has a passion for CliftonStrengths® coaching and training. Denise is married to Joe and has four daughters, four sons-in-law, and eight grandchildren (so far!). Her favorite pastime is time spent with family.

Denise's Strength Contribution to the Book

It was definitely my **Connectedness** that fired up as we collaborated on this project. Seven unique voices, each with its own style, all attempting to unite in a cohesive whole – that entails a lot of **Connectedness**. Gallup® explains that people exceptionally talented in **Connectedness** have faith in the links among people and things. Without a doubt, I have faith in what links our team together: joy, caring, trust, love, respect, positivity, flexibility, creativity. It was a privilege to unite and celebrate our strengths as we fully harnessed the energy of a JoyPowered™ team.

joypowered

Appendix D: Bibliography

1. "Live Your Best Life Using CliftonStrengths®, " *Gallup®, Inc. 2018,*

   https://www.gallupstrengthscenter.com/?utm_source=g oogle&utm_medium=cpc&utm_campaign=Strengths_E Commerce_Brand_Search_US&utm_content=clifton%2 0strengths%20assessment&gclid=Cj0KCQiA5NPjBRDD ARIsAM9X1GJYG4Qw4AlfQMFc3l631FlYhMoXwUGNF upDZMyS9_1YEMGRWm1HdvkaAjwzEALw_wcB

2. Curtis, JoDee, *JoyPowered™: Intentionally Creating an Inspired Workspace* (New Jersey: BookBaby, 2016.)

3. Schmidt, Catherine, "Why Employees are a Team, Not a Family," Purple Ink LLC (Blog,) accessed February 6, 2019, https://purpleinkllc.com/2014/07/31/why-employees-are-a-team-not-a-family/

4. Darby, Ryan, "What Is a Strengths-Based Team?," *Gallup®, Inc.,* December 12, 2012, http://coaching.gallup.com/2012/12/what-is-strengths-based-team.html

5. Asplund, Jim and Blacksmith, Nikki, "The Secret of Higher Performance: How integrating employee engagement and strengths boosts both," *Gallup®, Inc.,* May 3, 2011,

   https://news.gallup.com/businessjournal/147383/secret-higher-performance.aspx

6. Burchard, Brendon, *High Performance Habits* (California: Hay House Inc., 2017.)

7. Collins, Jim, *Good to Great: Why Some Companies Make the Leap…and Others Don't* (New York: Harper-Collins Publishers, 2001.)

8. Sharma, Robin, "How To Build A Winning Team – 5 Best Team Building Practices." YouTube video, 6:18. April 20, 2011, accessed February 6, 2019, https://www.youtube.com/watch?v=ckEOQKmZPlI

9. Dungy, Tony, *The Mentor Leader: Secrets to Building People and Teams That Win Consistently* (Illinois: Tyndale Momentum, 2011)

10. Angeles, Domingo, "Younger baby boomers and number of jobs held," *Bureau of Labor Statistics,* June 2016, https://www.bls.gov/careeroutlook/2016/data-on-display/younger-baby-boomers-and-number-of-jobs-held.htm

11. Cain, Susan, *Quiet: The Power of Introverts in a World That Can't Stop Talking* (New York: Broadway Books, 2013)

12. Hong, Lu and Page, Scott E. *Proceedings of the National Academy of the Sciences.* 2004. Accessed April 10, 2019. https://sites.lsa.umich.edu/scottepage/wp-content/uploads/sites/344/2015/11/pnas.pdf

13. Rock, David and Grant, Heidi, "Why Diverse Teams Are Smarter," *Harvard Business Review,* November 4, 2016, accessed January 10, 2019, https://hbr.org/2016/11/why-diverse-teams-are-smarter

14. Kelley, Tom with Littman, Jonathan, *The Art of Innovation: Lessons in Creativity from IDEO, America's Leading Design Firm* (New York: Doubleday, 1995)

15. Wilber, Rachelle, "Engaged Employees: How Diversity Improves Workplace Morale" *HR.com,* July 15, 2015, accessed January 10, 2019, https://www.hr.com/en/app/blog/2015/07/engaged-employees-how-diversity-improves-workplace_icp73cba.html

16. "Charge Statistics for Discrimination and Harassment Show Unsettling Trend," *Healthcare Compliance Pros,* http://www.healthcarecompliancepros.com/blog/charge_stats_for_discrimination_and_harassment_trend/

17. Amy Chua, *Political Tribes: Group Instinct and the Fate of Nations* (New York, Penguin Random House LLC, 2018).

18. Noon, Mike, "Pointless Diversity Training: Unconscious Bias, New Racism and Agency," *Sage Journals,* September 1, 2017. accessed January 10, 2019, https://doi.org/10.1177/0950017017719841

19. Taking Action Against Racism in the Media, s.v. "Microaggressions," 2007, accessed January 10, 2019, https://www.div17.org/TAAR/media/topics/microaggressions.php

20. Shrock, Saundra, "SHRM Credit: Diversity in the Workspace," Purple Ink LLC (Podcast,) https://joypowered.podbean.com/e/shrm-credit-diversity-in-the-workspace/

21. Dr. Upton, Sandra, "A Black Woman's Advice to White Professionals." The Cultural Intelligence Center (Blog), 2017, accessed January 10, 2019, https://culturalq.com/a-black-womans-advice-to-white-professionals/

22. Bolden-Barrett, Valerie, "Hilton tops Best Workplaces for Diversity list," *HR Dive,* December 10, 2018, accessed December 28, 2018, https://www.hrdive.com/news/hilton-tops-best-workplaces-for-diversity-list/543916/

23. "How to Increase Workplace Diversity," *Wall Street Journal*, April 7, 2009, accessed December 28, 2018, http://guides.wsj.com/management/building-a-workplace-culture/how-to-increase-workplace-diversity/

24. Lorenzo, Rocío, "How diversity makes teams more innovative." TED video, 11:06. "TED Conferences, LLC," October 2017, https://www.ted.com/talks/rocio_lorenzo_want_a_more_innovative_company_hire_more_women

25. Hwang, Rebeca, "The power of diversity within yourself," TED video, 9:45. "TED Conferences, LLC," April 2018, https://www.ted.com/talks/rebeca_hwang_the_power_of_diversity_within_yourself

26. Sinek, Simon, "Why good leaders make you feel safe." TED video, 11:56. "TED Conferences, LLC," March 2014, accessed February 1, 2018, https://www.ted.com/talks/simon_sinek_why_good_leaders_make_you_feel_safe/up-next

27. Carucci, Ron, "When Companies Should Invest in Training Their Employees – and When They Shouldn't," *Harvard Business Review,* October 29, 2018, accessed January 31, 2019, https://hbr.org/2018/10/when-companies-should-invest-in-training-their-employees-and-when-they-shouldnt

28. Forbes Coaches Council, "13 Reasons To Offer Leadership Training And Development To Millennials," *Forbes,* December 22, 2017, accessed February 8, 2019, https://www.forbes.com/sites/forbescoachescouncil/2017/12/22/13-reasons-to-offer-leadership-training-and-development-to-millennials/#321f51737a14

29. "Recency Effect," *Psychology Research and Reference,* accessed January 31, 2019, https://psychology.iresearchnet.com/social-psychology/decision-making/recency-effect/

30. Murphy, Mark, "Fewer Than Half of Employees Know If They're Doing A Good Job," *Forbes,* September 4, 2016, accessed January 30, 2019, https://www.forbes.com/sites/markmurphy/2016/09/04/fewer-than-half-of-employees-know-if-theyre-doing-a-good-job/#130206741b32

31. "Jack Welch 1935- Biography forum," *Reference for Business, Advameg, Inc.,* Accessed January 31, 2019, https://www.referenceforbusiness.com/biography/S-Z/Welch-Jack-1935.html

32. Welch, Jack, with Welch, Suzy, *Winning: The Ultimate Business How-To Book* (New York: HarperCollins Publishers, 2005.)

33. "SHRM Research: Flexible Work Arrangements." *Society for Human Resource Management,* 2015, accessed February 7, 2019, https://www.shrm.org/hr-today/trends-and-forecasting/special-reports-and-expert-views/Documents/Flexible%20Work%20Arrangements.pdf

34. Miller, Emily, "4 Ways To Make Your Workplace More Flexible," Purple Ink LLC (Blog,) December 7, 2018, accessed January 31, 2019, https://purpleinkllc.com/2018/12/12/4-ways-to-make-your-workplace-more-flexible/

35. Pink, Daniel H., *Drive: The Surprising Truth About What Motivates Us* (New York: The Penguin Group, 2009.)

36. Bresciani, Alessio, "51 Mission Statement Examples from The World's Best Companies," *Alessio Bresciani,* accessed January 31, 2019, https://www.alessiobresciani.com/foresight-strategy/51-mission-statement-examples-from-the-worlds-best-companies/

37. Boss, Jeff, "Why Some Teams Fail And Others Prevail," *Forbes*, December 22, 2015, accessed December 10, 2019, https://www.forbes.com/sites/jeffboss/2015/12/22/why-some-teams-fail-and-others-prevail/

38. Miller, Emily, "The Power of Failure," Purple Ink LLC (Blog,) September 14, 2016, accessed December 8, 2018, https://purpleinkllc.com/2016/09/14/the-power-of-failure/

39. Lencioni, Patrick, *The Five Dysfunctions of a Team: A Leadership Fable* (San Francisco: Jossey Bass, 2002).

40. Curtis, JoDee, "How to Know When It's Time to Let Go," Purple Ink LLC (Blog,) September 1, 2016, accessed December 8, 2018, https://purpleinkllc.com/2016/09/01/how-to-know-when-its-time-to-let-go/

41. Wakeman, Cy, *No Ego: How Leaders Can Cut the Cost of Workplace Drama, End Entitlement, and Drive Big Results* (New York: St. Martin's Press, 2017)

42. Bensi, Mike, *The Success of Failure: A Coming-of-Age Fable About Overcoming Failure Despite Ourselves* (New York: Morgan James Publishing, 2017)

43. Bensi, Mike, "A Leader's Response to Failure,"*Purple Ink LLC (Blog,)* May 30, 2018, accessed December 8, 2018, https://purpleinkllc.com/2018/05/30/a-leaders-response-to-failure/

44. Forbes Coaches Council, "14 Warning Signs That your Team Is Nearing Dysfunction," *Forbes,* 2016, https://www.forbes.com/sites/forbescoachescouncil/2016/08/26/14-warning-signs-that-your-team-is-nearing-dysfunction/#11175d2e6bd5

45. Mackey, John and Tindell, Kip, "Former housemates John Mackey and Kip Tindell talk about poker, retailing, and the limitations of shareholder capitalism," *Time USA, LLC,* June 26, 2008, http://business.time.com/2008/06/26/former_housemates_john_mackey/

46. "Gallup® Webcast: Building Employee Engagement Through High-Performing Managers." YouTube video, 50:26. Gallup® Employee Engagement Center, 2014. https://www.youtube.com/watch?v=CSjf156wx2o

47. Pink, Daniel, "Driving Employee Engagement." YouTube video, 23:41. "VitalSmarts Video," 2013, https://www.youtube.com/watch?v=x8PsRWvJz00

48. "Put People First, The VitalSmarts Approach," VitalSmarts, 2018, https://www.vitalsmarts.com/our-approach/

49. "How Millennials Want to Work and Live," Gallup®, Inc., 2016, https://news.gallup.com/reports/189830/e.aspx

50. Dimock, Michael, "Defining generations: Where Millennials end and Generation Z begins," *Pew Research Center,* January 17., 2019, http://www.pewresearch.org/fact-tank/2019/01/17/where-millennials-end-and-generation-z-begins/

51. Hsieh, Tony, *Delivering Happiness: A Path to Profits, Passion, and Purpose* (New York: Hachette Book Group, 2010)

52. Sheridan, Richard, *Joy, Inc.: How We Built a Workplace People Love* (New York: Penguin Random House, 2015.)

53. *Menlo Innovations,* https://menloinnovations.com

54. Hall, John, "11 Simple Ways To Show Your Employees You Care," *Forbes Media LLC,* https://www.forbes.com/sites/johnhall/2014/03/10/11-simple-ways-to-show-your-employees-you-care/#23da79ca450e

55. Col 3:14 (Saint Benedict Press; New American Bible Revised Edition edition)

56. Sheridan, Richard, *Chief Joy Officer: How Great Leaders Elevate Human Energy and Eliminate Fear* (New York: Penguin Random House, 2018)

57. 1 Cor 13:4-7 (Saint Benedict Press; New American Bible Revised Edition edition)

58. J. Grenny, D. Maxfield, K. Patterson, A. Switzler, and R. McMillan, *Influencer: The Power to Change Anything* (McGraw-Hill, 2013)

59. Adkins, Amy and Rigoni, Brandon, "Millennials Want Jobs to Be Development Opportunities," *Gallup®, Inc.,* June 30, 2016, https://www.gallup.com/workplace/236438/millennials-jobs-development-opportunities.aspx

60. Hyacinth, Brigette Tasha, *The Future of Leadership: Rise of Automation, Robotics and Artificial Intelligence*, Publisher: MBA Caribbean Organisation; 1 edition (October 6, 2017)

61. "Employee Tenure Summary." *Bureau of Labor Statistics,* September 20, 2018, Accessed April 10, 2019. https://www.bls.gov/news.release/tenure.nr0.htm

62. Kubler-Ross, E. and Kessler, D., *On Grief and Grieving: Finding the Meaning of Grief Through the Five Stages of Loss* (New York: Simon & Schuster, 2005.)

63. Bauer, Talya N., "Onboarding New Employees: Maximizing Success." SHRM Foundation, 2010, accessed November 11, 2018, https://www.shrm.org/foundation/ourwork/initiatives/resources-from-past-initiatives/Documents/Onboarding%20New%20Employees.pdf

64. Spiegelman, Paul, "Why You Need to Fire Bad Employees Right Now." Inc.com, December 11, 2014, accessed November 11, 2018, https://www.inc.com/paul-spiegelman/employers-dont-have-the-courage-to-fire-bad-employees.html.

65. "State of the American Workplace," Gallup®, Inc, 2017, accessed November 11, 2018, Gallup's 2017, https://www.gallup.com/workplace/238085/state-american-workplace-report-2017.aspx

joypowered